About the Author

James Hemming was a teacher for a number of years, during which he became increasingly critical of the dominant educational process. The better to sift the matter, he went on to take an honours degree and doctorate in psychology and turned his attention to educational research, writing, and work in industrial relations and counselling, which gave him the opportunity to meet young people in a variety of situations. He has lectured around the world, participated in educational advance in Africa, and has broadcast on many occasions at home and overseas. Among various public activities, he is educational adviser to the World Education Fellowship and President of the British Humanist Association.

Acknowledgements

I would like to express my grateful thanks to the teachers, students and friends who have contributed to the content of this book, to Elizabeth Blackaby for her assistance with research, and to my wife, Kay, who has helped in many ways, not least in typing the manuscript and reading the proofs.

About the Series

IDEAS IN PROGRESS is a commercially published series of working papers dealing with alternatives to industrial society. It is our belief that the ills and profound frustrations which have overtaken man are not merely due to industrial civilization's inadequate planning and faulty execution, but are caused by fundamental errors in our basic thinking about goals. This series is designed to question and rethink the underlying concepts of many of our institutions and to propose alternatives. Unless this is done soon, society will undoubtedly create even greater injustice and inequalities than it contains at present. It is to correct this trend that authors are invited to submit short monographs of work in progress of interest not only to their colleagues but also to the general public. The series fosters direct contact between the author and the reader. It provides the author with the opportunity to give wide circulation to his draft while he is still developing an idea. It offers the reader an opportunity to participate critically in shaping this idea before it has taken on a definite form. Future editions of this paper may include the author's revisions and critical reactions from the public. Readers are invited to write directly to the author of the present volume at the following address: James Hemming, 31 Broom Water, Teddington, Middlesex TW11 9QJ, England.

THE PUBLISHERS

THE BETRAYAL OF YOUTH

IDEAS IN PROGRESS

THE BETRAYAL OF YOUTH

Secondary Education Must be Changed

James Hemming

MARION BOYARS
LONDON · BOSTON

First published in Great Britain and the United States in 1980
By Marion Boyars Publishers Ltd.
18 Brewer Street, London W1R 4AS
and
Marion Boyars Publishers Inc.
99 Main Street, Salem, New Hampshire 03079

Australian distribution by Thomas C. Lothian
4–12 Tattersalls Lane, Melbourne, Victoria 3000

British Library Cataloguing in Publication Data

Hemming, James
    The betrayal of youth. – (Ideas in progress).
    1. Education, Secondary
    I. Title II. Series
    373   LB1607

ISBN 0–7145–2692–4 Cased edition
      0–7145–2693–2 Paperback edition

Library of Congress Catalog Card Number 79–56848

Printed and bound in Great Britain by
REDWOOD BURN LIMITED
Trowbridge & Esher

CONTENTS

If the mind of man gets its nourishment, there is nothing which will not grow. If it loses its nourishment, there is nothing that will not perish.

Mencius on education

One had to cram all this stuff into one's mind for the examinations, whether one liked it or not. This coercion had such a deterring effect on me that, after I passed the final examination, I found the consideration of any scientific problems distasteful to me for an entire year.

Albert Einstein on cramming

'I can't say I've got something out of school because I haven't got much at all because the things I need I didn't get, like maths and English. I got woodwork but that's about all I got out of it but actually I didn't get nothing else. It's been a hard time for me.'

One modern adolescent on his schooling

1

THE BACKGROUND

Around the world, a debate is going on about how we ought
to educate our adolescents. What should we teach them? By
what methods? To attain what ends? Judged by what standards? Assessed by what tests? Should the development of
the individual be our chief concern, or preparation for voca-
tional and social roles? Is it possible to do justice to all at
once?

Meanwhile the adolescents themselves are victims of the
confusion of aims. At the top end of the hierarchy of scholastic ability the more able are subjected to pressure which
is out of tune with the sensitive developmental years of
adolescence and produces stress up to the ultimate despair
of suicide or the desperate cry for help of parasuicide, and
includes the various escape routes of dropping-out, drugs,
drink, and the rest. At the other extreme, the defeated
rejects of the system sit out their schooldays in moods rang-
ing from bored apathy to open hostility and leave school
with their confidence and curiosity shattered, their powers
of concentration atrophied, and a bitter hatred in their hearts
for the society which has put them down.

Of course not all students become over-stressed or give
up. A proportion thrive on what their schools have to offer.
Others, while going through the routines of the classroom
without much zest, enjoy the friendships and the general
facilities that school life provides. But success in school, or
being happy there, does not necessarily ensure the overall
development of potentialities, competence and personality
which the schools exist to achieve, and which the young

people themselves need. Both the provision and outcome are, often, of a lower quality than they ought to be, or need be.

It is not that the schools and the teachers are not trying. They are, and many of them very hard. Some schools achieve miracles, become havens of happy relationships and fulfilled growth to which the students go willingly and which they leave as well-balanced individuals, with their self-esteem intact, prepared to tackle the challenges of adult life. But education of this type – the sort that *every* adolescent has the right to expect – is attained in spite of the system rather than because of it. The weakness of the system is that it is not sufficiently concerned about individual development. It is too much tied up with routines of teaching and testing, accepting and rejecting. Consequently it has proved highly resistant to making the necessary fundamental changes.

But the system must change now. The sort of future we are moving into makes the change imperative. But to begin with we must first clarify the purpose of secondary education. People talk as if this were a great problem; actually it is unequivocally simple. The job of secondary education is to nourish the positive potentialities of *every* individual, to develop personal competence, to offer opportunities for exercising responsibility, to foster moral insight, to give a perspective on society and the world, and to prepare for adulthood – all within a purposeful, friendly social environment that keeps curiosity and confidence alive and gives plenty of openings for exciting involvement.

Too tall an order? Loading too much on the schools? If it is, then we really had better give up schools and try some other approach to education as some, indeed, have already suggested. The future that is staring adolescents in the face will make all sorts of unexpected demands on them and will call for higher levels of self-assured, integrated development than we are at present achieving. Young people currently in school will shortly be involved in both shaping the future and adapting to it. The sort of end-stopped education we now offer them – learn, pass your tests, and throw away your books – will not do. In the future, education will need

2

to be life-long. Those who are not flexible enough to relearn, nor curious enough to keep in touch, nor sufficiently equipped with inner resources to deal with extended leisure, nor socially skilled enough to make friends wherever they find themselves will be stuck and isolated before they are middle-aged. The young are already in the new era insofar as the future is alive in the present. They are getting the scent of it. They intuitively feel that some vital element is missing in the education to which they are being subjected. They complain of 'irrelevance' about what they are expected to learn. Schooling, all too often, fails to give them a sense of growth, emergence, becoming adult. Many feel that their schooling is holding them back from life. So the need for change becomes ever more obvious.

The key to advance in secondary education does not primarily lie in new curricula, new methods, new systems of assessing and accountability – much as these urgently need attention – but in transformed attitudes to the adolescents themselves. Adolescents want to make a success of their lives. But they cannot function effectively in a system that does not take account of their needs and natures as young adults. Secondary education is not, as a system, a milieu in which adolescents can flourish because it is not designed to suit *them*; rather, they have to fit as best they may into a framework of activities and demands which is imposed by habits of the past, and by authorities over which they have no control. This state of affairs is out of date. The schools and the adolescents have to get nearer to one another. A major reason why secondary education has lagged behind in a period of explosive social change is that it has cut itself off too much from the most constructive feed-back available to it – the feed-back from the nature, needs and aspirations of the adolescents themselves. The young people sense this disregard for their personal lives and the level of motivation for their schooling drops. No one can feel identified with a system that does not really seem to care about the individual. Industry and the other institutions of technological society are slowly coming to accept the inevitability of this human truth. Education must accept it too.

The other big gap between the educational needs of adolescents and traditional secondary schooling arises from the neglect by the secondary system of the psychodynamic principles of human development. It is an extraordinary fact that the dominant influences operating in secondary education have no scientific basis whatever. They arise from dubitable philosophical ideas that had their origin in the distant past – the Greek view that the craftsman was inherently inferior to the thinker; Locke's presentation of the mind as a clean slate, a '*tabula rasa*'; Descartes' over-evaluation of the intellect, and his division of the human being into mind (exalted) and body (debased); puritan ideas about the special value of making the young do what they don't like doing, plus the more recent influence arising from academic confusion between knowledge and competence. Young people are constantly having their confidence and courage broken on one or another of the distortions of the educational truth.

Now that we have at our disposal knowledge of brain functioning and the principles of personal development, which did not exist when the habits of thought were generated which still control much of secondary education, we are in a greatly improved position to base our education more soundly. With extraordinary myopia, the secondary system goes on its way as if these principles had never been discovered, or it exists in a confused state in which modern developmental principles and old habits of thought are constantly in conflict with one another. The result is an appalling loss of vigour and waste of time – for both pupils and teachers.

Of course, it is not only the schools that frustrate adolescent development. Society in general does. Bad housing, drab environments, overcrowding, lack of appropriate outlets for adolescent energy and the brutal social rejection of unemployment inhibit the positive potentialities of young people, but whereas social improvements take a long time, schools can quickly change so as to serve the growth of adolescents better, if they have a will to do so. Furthermore, self-confident, competent, young people, developed in the round, will themselves help to promote the necessary social

4

changes, by their determined involvement in affairs, in a way which academic aloofness or hostile apathy can never hope to achieve. In fact, the challenge of the future will need to be matched by a higher quality of personal education. Already problems are outdistancing capability. We have to release more human potential to balance the account.

This book is concerned with how to stimulate the dynamic of young people and how to counter those forces and influences in the prevailing secondary school system which distort, or crush, that dynamic. The solutions to our problems lie in cooperation with what the young *are*; lacking that, no amount of ingenuity in curriculum design will save us from abusing the capabilities of our adolescents and reducing many of them to hostility and despair. In the next chapter, by way of background, we shall consider some of the basic drives of adolescents and how in simple societies – though not in our sort of society – these drives are used to develop maturity and responsibility in the young. I am not doing this in order to suggest that we should copy the past – we are in a quite new situation with our modern adolescents and the unpredictable future they face – but in order to present a contrast of climates for adolescent growth, one of which readily accepts the young as they are and lets them develop as themselves and the other, our own, which is more inclined to regard them as inevitably awkward, unmanageable and irresponsible. Adolescents can, of course, be cussed, but their cussedness is usually provoked.

2

ATTAINING ADULTHOOD

It is the dearest wish of every adolescent to attain significant adulthood and to receive social recognition of that status. The very existence of secondary schools is at present a hazard to this because the secondary school system coincides with those years in which the young are longing to escape from the tutelage of childhood. But far from the school developing the dignity of adulthood it seems set upon withholding it from them. Some find schooling more irksome as the years pass, particularly girls it seems, according to the Schools Council's *Enquiry 1*. Even senior pupils, in spite of the relaxation of 'pettifogging rules', may live in an ambivalent state of appreciating what they are gaining from the school while getting more and more restless at what they feel to be restrictions on their maturity. One student, now in first-year at university, summed up this feeling: 'I don't think I could have stood another term of it,' an attitude which has been echoed in many pop songs. Resentment at feeling held back from adult status no doubt accounts for the increasing number of those young people who prefer to do their final years of secondary education in colleges of further education.

The way that the schools fail to reach the young in terms of their eagerness to grow up leads to recurring waste. Pupils who leave school early, and with a sigh of relief, eager to get their teeth into the real business of living, often, after quite a short time, belatedly see the advantages of school and wish they had made more use of their opportunities while they were there. (Sweden, incidentally, recognizes this and makes it possible to 'drop back in' without difficulty.)

This all leads to a serious motivation gap that makes things unnecessarily difficult both for the schools and their students. The origin of the gap is a failure on the part of the secondary system to use the actual psychodynamics of adolescence to bring about the growth in responsibility, maturity and sense of adulthood which, as research shows, parents, teachers and students all see as important aims of education. What you cannot possibly do is to run the world of the classroom as an authoritarian system in which the pupils have no significant role except to submit, and, at the same time, bring the energies of the students to a focus in the service of their own education. Either what is offered for learning must be experienced by the adolescents as illuminating, and informing their own life purposes, or it will be, at best, tolerated and, at worst, rejected. Often students see their studies almost entirely in terms of the price that has to be paid for future status. But here too, the immediate goals of the adolescent's life are not incorporated in what is going on as the incentives tied up with them are lost.

This schizoid state of affairs in the classroom is damaging. It dilutes application, makes concentration more difficult, constantly reinforces the idea that school and personal life are poles apart and undermines respect for the culture and values the school seeks to represent. (We will not here go into the thorny issue of the school foisting 'middle class values' on its students. There are elements in any culture which are classless and universally desirable, just as there are human values which have to be respected in *any* society if it is to survive. These, obviously, the school should foster.)

It is in this matter of utilizing the immediate nature, needs and aspirations of adolescents to further their growth to responsible adulthood that we may well have something to learn from the initiation techniques of simple societies which are remarkably successful in achieving this. But, first, we must take a look at the psychodynamics of the adolescent stage of life.

Adolescence is an explosion of development. The body increases rapidly in size and weight, providing a greater

7

muscular strength, the urge to use it, and the energy to put it to use. A flood of hormones emphasize sexual differentiation, bring physical maturity, and intensify consciousness of one's own sexuality, and the attractions of sex. Emotions deepen and expand. Aesthetic sensitivity sharpens. Intelligence attains its maximum capacity. The need to acquire social skills is urgently experienced, as are also the longings for prestige and recognition as independent adults. Identity has to be searched for and understood when found. And with that come all the problems of relating, as oneself, to others – finding out where one comes in the social group. Somehow a dependable framework of values needs to be discovered as a guide to life and a basis for decisions.

Although interest about sexual relationships is only one of the absorbing concerns of adolescents, it provides a good example of the school's tendency to exclude as irrelevant or peripheral what to the adolescent is relevant and central. A Deputy Headmistress who is herself much concerned about the gap between school life and life *within the minds of the students themselves* illustrated her point by giving me a used rough book which one of the staff had handed to her. The owner of the book is a bright adolescent girl of 13 – Juliet's age incidentally. She gets 12 out of 13 for a Biology test and 15 out of 19 for English. What interested the Deputy Head was the evidence of split motivation that the book provided.

Page one is fully taken up with a neatly set out time–table of the girl's studies. Page two starts with a Chemistry test under which is written BRIAN IS GREAT. On the next page, under a note on Religious Studies, she uses up a quarter of the page with a design composed of the two words BRIAN and GREAT. At the bottom of the page is what looks like an irreverent comment on the teacher for the benefit of her classmate: 'Her teeth are gonna fall out any minute.' And, in the margin, there is more evidence of the underground communication system: 'Coming to the shop after school? I'll buy you a lollipop.'

So it goes on throughout the book. By page six we have I LOVE BRIAN but PETE and SID also get attention in ornate lettering. There follows, close to another Biology test

8

bristling with ticks, more evidence of the bush telegraph; this time, obviously, a reply to a friend's communication: 'His lips are always wet and slobbery. You'd need a towel.'

Boy friends come and go until, by the end of the book, among some well-executed fashion drawings, we are introduced to the girl's current set of friends: 'I don't half like Tim. When he and Steve came up to Chris and I, and he groaned and pulled me towards him, he started sort of necking with me, and I was sort of kneading his stomach to make him feel better. Then Ron came up and said "Can anyone watch?" '

This girl is obviously a bright, alert young person who is getting plenty of achievement from the curriculum she is following with marked success – a good university candidate in the making. But her private world – her more valued world? – is impinging all the time on the encapsulated teach-and-test of school which has no means of forming a rapprochement with her maturing womanhood. If this dual motivation appears in an able girl, what is likely to be happening to a boy or girl who cannot cope with the curriculum and is becoming more and more alienated from it? How is such a student to establish a sense of identity with the school or to acquire a sense of personal worth from it? We can ask that question about many of the prime motivations of adolescents: for achievement, recognition, responsibility, social success, new experiences, adventure, excitement, understanding of life and the rest.

The problem of the school, as the Deputy Head pointed out, is to accept the existence of the pupils' private worlds and to form a bridge between them and what the school has to offer. 'They don't regard school as about life,' she said. 'School is a different sort of activity.' For girls, especially around 14–15, because of their earlier maturation, relations with the other sex are an absorbing interest. In what ways does the classroom acknowledge this?

A major need of the young is a sense of significance. Lacking this they are uneasy and restless. Adolescent boys in particular, if they do not feel they can make their mark in socially useful attainment will, as Alfred Adler pointed out long ago, turn, as compensation, to some ostentatious alternative of a socially useless, or even damaging, kind. Vandalism is the self-expression of despair. And in recent years we have seen an increase of this tendency in girls.

Simple societies understood the need of the young for sexual expression along with personal recognition and appreciation, and established initiation training and ceremonies which both prepared the individuals for adulthood and also provided a dramatic way of giving young people convincing proof that they were accepted as responsible adults. They brought the main absorptions of adolescence together as a focus of maturation. Our sophisticated societies have, in contrast, notably failed in this and are continuing to fail.

Lack of balance between learning and life, between personal development and formal academic goals, not only estranges the young but imposes an unnecessary burden on teachers. There is no more disheartening or undignified human employment than that of the teacher who feels obliged to try to teach material that young people can see no point in learning and who become more and more unmanageable as the attempt proceeds.

Against this background, let us now take a look at the adolescent training systems which were used by simple societies before the impact of the West – and, in some instances, are still used – to help young people to find their feet confidently in the adult world. Some of these systems were pretty tough, even gruesome – the clitorectomy of girls for example. But they worked, and their principles, though not their practices, are as valid today as ever they were.

The systems worked for four reasons: they accepted the physical robustness and sexuality of adolescents; they used these to train the young people in a whole range of life skills; they ended by giving the young people the assurance of valued adulthood along with a clear perspective on themselves; *and nobody was rejected*. The prestige and kudos that went with official acceptance to adult membership of the tribe was to be anticipated by all and was achieved by all. Professor Philip Mayer and Dr Iona Mayer in their paper

'The Youth Organizations of the Red Xhosa' have given us a picture of one such system which warrants careful study by Western educators.

The adolescent group in Xhosa society, say from thirteen to the early twenties, takes on the form of a self-regulating youth organization. This includes vigorous fighting games, shared social life, and approved premarital sexual relationships. To avoid the risks of unwanted pregnancy, sexual intercourse excludes penetration, not for moralistic reasons but because an unmarried mother would not fit anywhere into adult society and would be a lonely and unhappy person.

The Mayers do not make it clear what technique the Xhosa use to prevent impregnation, but Jomo Kenyatta, the late President of Kenya, gives us, in *Facing Mount Kenya*, the method used by the young Kikuyu: 'The boy removes all his clothing. The girl removes her upper garment and retains her skirt and her soft leather apron, which she pulls back between her legs and tucks in together with her leather skirt. The two V-shaped tails of her skirt are pulled forward between her legs from behind and fastened to the waist thus keeping her apron in position and forming an effective protection of her private parts.' (It is interesting to note that sleeping together without full intercourse or, indeed, just for the cuddly companionship of it, is now accepted as a perfectly normal mode of sexual relationship among some adolescents who look upon the notion that intercourse is a *necessary* concomitant of sleeping together as an adult hang-up.)

The fighting games of Xhosa youth give even the most pugnacious adolescent all the aggro he could possibly want. Every youth carries two fighting sticks, or light clubs, one shorter than the other, and may challenge any of his comrades to an encounter provided that the contestants are fairly matched and of approximately equal skill. Fights are not 'to the death' but terminate as soon as one or the other accepts defeat. The older adolescents supervise one another's fights and train the younger ones in correct fighting techniques and etiquette. Team contests between groups or villages are sometimes arranged. Girls may fight one another if they wish

11

to do so, but they do not join in the boys' contests. No one is forced to fight and care is taken to avoid serious injury. On the whole, the fighting games carry little more risk to life and limb than, say, rugby football. Grudges may also be settled by a fight, following the accepted rules.

Social expertise is developed through parties and dances and through more serious group meetings, organized by the young people themselves. The Mayers tell us: 'These groups provide a forum where male youth acquire politicojudicial skills and develop a concern with "law" – both highly valued in Red Xhosa culture. In these groups social contacts with peers are progressively widened, in a way that makes for eventual self-identification as a Xhosa, over and above kinship and community identification.'

The dances of the young Xhosa and their sexual lives fit naturally together. At the dances, it is considered bad manners for the pretty girls and handsome young men to monopolize each other; a dance is a group occasion for everyone to enjoy. Who sleeps with whom when the dancing is over is a mutual choice but is ultimately in control of the girls. Each girl takes a decorated stick to the dance. This she shares with each boy in the line of dancers but takes it back again until she comes opposite to her 'best boy friend'. He is allowed to hold the decorated stick for the rest of the dance. Another sign of intimacy is for the girl to take off the towel she wears around her waist and wipe the sweat from her lover's face with it. In this way everyone knows who is going with whom.

Sexual behaviour is self-regulating within the group. Having more than one lover at the same time is frowned upon. The older girls instruct the younger ones in the art of making love without penetration. If any young male makes himself troublesome by trying to impregnate a girl, she warns the other girls and he is liable to find himself without a partner until he mends his ways. It is not all perfect, but it works out pretty well. (Incidentally, all the unpleasant signs of sexual inadequacy that plague the West – trivial sex, illegitimacy, flashing, rape, child molestation, obscenity – are virtually unknown in Xhosa society and others like it.)

12

When the Xhosa elders decide that the time is ripe for a young man to undertake adult responsibilities – between the ages of 18 and 23 – he is invited to join the next group of initiates for the final rituals and ceremonies after which he is given 'a flattering reception by adult society' and is thereafter expected to take on the roles of a junior adult. Following initiation, the young man hangs up his clubs because 'Only boys settle things with the stick.' From henceforward disputes are to be reasoned out by discussion and, if necessary, legal process. The girl friends accompany the boys in this progress of promotion into adult society.

The entire initiation phase offers a thorough training in many important life skills: self-reliance, mutual dependence, cooperation, responsibility, initiative, social acumen, consideration for others, communication, an understanding of society, and ability to relate sensitively to the other sex. It also gives clarity of self-perspective. Over the years each young man learns to recognize where he comes in the various hierarchies of speed, agility, quickness of thought, strength, courage, skill, the ability to lead or follow, and the rest. He therefore enters manhood knowing where he stands and freed from the compulsion constantly to test himself aggressively against others, which is something often found in our western societies.

It may seem that little is to be gained from this flash-back to tribal society. If, however, we look closely at the initiation process we see at once how comparatively insecure our own young people are. In place of an open-air life of constant excitement and adventure we coop our young adults up for hours of every school day, expecting them to pursue with enthusiasm comparatively dull routines of formal study. Overall, our young people are left to struggle their way towards maturity in an unstructured, haphazard manner which incites a good deal of exhibitionism in lieu of significant outlets. What are the significant outlets for the ordinary adolescent who cannot compete in the meritocracy race? Where are the opportunities to face and master challenges, *within the range of their powers*?

Another difficulty for our young people is to know for sure

when they *have* arrived. Simple societies offered a clear dividing line between adolescence and adulthood – 'a total status change' as the Mayers put it. In Western society the vestigial remains of the initiation system can still be seen: the kudos of passing exams, graduation ceremonies, and the like. But all of these are piecemeal and selective so that self-respect and adult status are left in the air. Manhood and womanhood come by inches – the age of consent, the age for a driving licence, the voting age, the first job, marriage and so forth. This is, no doubt, inevitable but it does make it difficult for the young to know exactly when they are accepted as mature and responsible adults.

The situation is made worse by the intolerance of adults as a whole towards adolescent sexuality. In primitive society, adolescent sexuality is welcomed as a means of helping to civilize young people and of developing their responsibility towards one another. In our society, even though we are supposed to be in a permissive age, sexual activity among adolescents is frowned upon. It follows that adolescents feel they cannot share the truth of their sexual lives with the adults around them; consequently they tend to be either secretive or brashly exhibitionist.

An equal gap in understanding is to be noticed in the unwillingness of adult society either to accept, or provide outlets for, the abundant robust physical energy of adolescents. Games are helpful, but not all young people are good at games, or like them. One of the Governors of Maidstone Gaol set out to find what were the interests of his youthful charges. One young man, when asked what his hobby was, replied 'Climbing tall buildings.' The young man used the façades of factories to stand in for natural rocks and cliffs. We have to accept that our healthy, vigorous young people are desperately short of appropriate outlets for their energies and that, until something is done to remedy this, we must not be surprised if many of them make nuisances of themselves for no other reason than frustration and boredom.

It is not easy to formulate a modern equivalent of initiation ceremonies but it is at least a start to recognize the role they played in the transition from childhood to adulthood and to seek to make up for the loss of the help they gave to young people. How can we make the adolescent years more mobile, robust, adventurous and exciting? Would a year away from home between school and work, or school and higher education, help if there were a wide variety of opportunities on offer? How can we acknowledge the adolescents' emergence into adulthood by doing things *with* them rather than *to* them, and by drawing them into responsibility for their own education and development? How can we help them to feel good about themselves as people, in spite of the wide range of differing abilities and personalities within the adolescent group? How can we give them the assurance of being worthwhile individuals with a valued contribution to make to adult society?

Up to the present, secondary education has not got far in answering such questions. It is not difficult to see why this is so. There are scores of good schools, dedicated teachers, imaginative inspectors. However, their struggle is for ever against the stream because, owing to an historical accident, or series of accidents, secondary education has remained too much caught up in a self-perpetuating system which separates schooling from life and leaves the actual powers of the adolescents themselves largely untapped. The cost for adolescents, educators and society is incalculable.

This chapter has been about the general situation of adolescents in their struggle to relate to adult society, and about the failure of school and society to provide the sort of help adolescents need if they are to reach self-confident maturity. But the points raised are only a beginning to what has to be done if secondary education is to shake off its past and become a system capable of drawing on, and drawing out, the growth potential of adolescents. Some of the other things that urgently need attention we shall consider in the following chapters. It is not possible to cover all aspects. The issues are too many and too complicated to be handled in full. I shall limit myself to the more damaging flaws in the system. The obvious place to start is with the dangers of over-emphasizing academic values in education.

3

THE ACADEMIC ILLUSION

For hundreds of years, the young of the nation who were fortunate enough to get any schooling at all struggled and suffered under the rigours of the classical illusion. 'I learnt Latin,' said Dr Samuel Johnson, 'because my master beat me well.' Dr Johnson was beaten and learnt his Latin, but thousands were beaten and did not learn theirs because only a few young people have the combination of ability and flair which is required to make a success of the classics. The unfortunate rest grew up to regard themselves as duffers, incapable of achieving what was, at the time, the socially acceptable proof of a cultivated mind – the ability to put together some limping stanzas of Latin verse, and to bring out the appropriate classical tag on demand.

This sort of divisive evaluation still persists but nowadays it affects the whole adolescent population while the source of being made to feel inferior is not the classical illusion but the academic illusion – the erroneous assumption that human quality is to be pre-eminently assessed in terms of intellectual ability; and intellectual ability, moreover, of a rather arid kind. This is a major flaw in secondary education. The academic style of learning is primarily concerned with the accumulation and memorization of facts, the grouping of concepts into specialisms, and the application of these facts and concepts to the solution of problems, usually of an abstract nature rather than ones involving a real-life encounter with things and people. Those who can play the academic game get the kudos and prizes while those who can't are pushed, sometimes gently, but always firmly, down the meritocracy ladder. It is a demoralizing experience to be forced onto the field of play when you are not good at the game.

The academic illusion bristles with other anti-educational consequences. By placing all the emphasis, and the prestige, on a single function of the mind it has distorted the entire educational process. What has twisted everything askew is not a proper respect for the intellect but the comparative neglect of all other important attributes of human beings such as 'the intelligence of feeling', aesthetic awareness, imagination, intuition, judgement, breadth of apprehension, initiative, creative capacity, relational skill, manual proficiency and capability in general affairs. The enemy of education is not a genuine regard for the intellect but arrogant intellectual élitism.

Unfortunately, through their grip on the examination machinery, the academics have a stranglehold on the entire secondary system. The top prizes in the meritocracy struggle are degrees and similar awards. How are these obtained? By playing the academic game the academic way. What about original thought? Candidates had better be careful. Non-conformity is frowned upon. In spite of the restructuring of some examinations and degrees, to make them more open and reality-based, memory and the successful reproduction of stored facts are still the royal road to university honours. In this situation, it is all too easy for the ceaseless struggle between the schools and the Examination Boards to dominate everything else.

The effects of the academic illusion percolate throughout secondary education and constantly invade the primary schools. Because the highest prizes of the system are academic, it is academic attainment upon which the schools focus most of their attention so that developmental values, which promote the nourishment and growth of whole, well-balanced personalities, are subordinated for most of the time to academic values. The backbone of secondary and higher education is a hierarchy of competitive tests which range from a first-class honours degree and then proceed, step by step, down the scale of academic attainment until we reach the meagre glory of one or two low-grade examination results. Below that come the adolescents who leave school with nothing to show for eleven years of compulsory education. Some authorities have mercifully, if belatedly, come to the rescue of these bottom-liners by sending them home with a Record of Personal Achievement. Though a help, this does not itself remove the most poisonous consequence of the whole system – that it generates failure.

The insidious spread of failure, and the sense of inferiority that goes with it, extend viciously over everything, a terror to students and teachers alike. Even an individual who expects a first-class honours degree and ends up with a second feels that he has had his weaknesses exposed, and so on all down the line.

To generate failure is to kill confidence. And confidence is the vitamin of human capability. This we can see in any face-to-face contest such as a tennis or chess match. So long as the confidence holds up, the potential of performance is high; if it crumples, skill becomes less precise and there may be a total functional collapse. Often the contest swings dramatically to and fro as first one, then the other, gains in confidence.

Furthermore, we have reason to believe that children tend to respond best to teachers who have confidence in them; when the teacher's expectation is high, pupils produce better results. Consequently, whenever academic values are dominant in a school, and in the minds of its teachers, the effect must be to erode confidence in the majority of the pupils. This is because only the top 25% of students, at most, in a non-selective school, can enhance their confidence by their encounter with the academic curriculum, while, in such a school, the attitude of the specialist teachers to the non-academic children is, often, to evaluate them not as individuals but as poor examination material. This sets up a vicious cycle in which low evaluation interacts with declining confidence to produce among the academically less able pupils a distaste for school and a sense of helplessness and hopelessness.

If we set this against the fact that all adolescents are searching for achievement and significance – they want to matter – we can see how, in those schools where it is obvious that academic success is the supreme criterion of value, the non-academics are forced to search for self-esteem in some other field than school life. The tempting area for boys is to use their muscles and cunning to get back at 'respectable society'. It is from the low-attainers that most of the hooliganism, vandalism, violence and delinquency come. Years ago, Sir Alec Clegg, when Director of Education for the West Riding of Yorkshire, warned that we should continue at our peril to neglect the developmental needs of the non-academic adolescents. No one paid much attention to his warnings and now we are faced with a sector of young barbarians that grows in numbers and menace year by year. These unfortunate young adults are unfulfilled in their own lives and a source of anxiety to everyone else. It is the academic illusion that has created these angry young men, many of whom have considerable untapped potentiality.

Motivation suffers badly in the over-academic school. All adolescents are interested in their own development but when growth is seen only in terms of scholastic success, then the basis for cooperation between the bulk of the students and their teachers is lost. Ideally, every period in every school for every child should give a sense of growth, and the experience of confidence through achievement. That ideal is unattainable, but the aim should be to get as near to it as possible. This is the only way to keep motivation high. No human being will pursue any activity for any length of time if it consistently brings more frustration than satisfaction. We can hardly expect adolescents to be more long-suffering in this regard than adults. Where academic values rule, frustration must be widely generated in any unselected group of adolescents.

The academic illusion defeats its own aims. Thinking about one's personal world is within the power of every normal child and should be encouraged. Good thinking is, presumably, close to the heart of the academic ideal. Yet the over-valuing of the academic style of thought – thinking about abstractions rather than thinking from within – produces in young people who are not of an academic bent a lack of assurance about their kind of thought. The experimental Social Studies course of Jerome Bruner and his colleagues organized around the theme 'Man' has as its first aim 'To give our pupils respect for and confidence in the powers of their own minds.' The academically oriented secondary school does not serve this aim for a majority of its pupils. Indeed, it has the opposite effect.

A visitor from overseas doing an Associateship at the London Institute of Education and, by his own choice, trying his hand with a class of fifteen-year-old non-examination pupils set the scene for the day's work by writing in huge capitals across the blackboard T H I N K, hopefully as an antidote to their purposeless disorder and silliness. In the slightly startled lull that greeted this opening gambit, one boy put up his hand and said: 'We're the no-gooders, Sir. We can't think.' That is what happens when academic success and the ability to think are treated as identical.

A great disadvantage of the academic illusion is that it leads to a one-dimensional approach to people and to experience. It perpetrates the error that feeling is anti-intellectual, whereas curiosity and zest – to name only two feelings – are powerful motivators in all creative science. Feeling, as even Descartes realized, is a part of thought. The cold intellect is another name for the dehumanized mind. Furthermore, a human being is not only a thinking creature but also an intuitive one. Leading scientists as well as artists have repeatedly stated that the leap into the unknown, the transforming innovation, comes as a sudden burst of illumination, usually following a long period of cogitating about the problem. After the new insight there comes more hard thinking to put in the logical infrastructure and make everything tidy and communicable. Thinking at its best then – creative thinking – is an amalgam of feeling, intuition and thought. Speaking of his struggle to get to grips with the laws of the cosmos, Einstein wrote: 'There is no logical path to these laws; only intuition, resting on sympathetic understanding, can lead to them.' Einstein said of his own creative powers, 'The really valuable thing is intuition.' In contrast, the academic tradition in education is indifferent to educating feeling and

20

intuition. It stays lock-stepped in its limited, and limiting, world of acquiring facts, memorizing them, and manipulating them to solve problems.

This leads on to yet another weakness of the academic tradition; it likes to operate by boxing up human knowledge into self-contained domains. This makes it an almost impossible task, for all but the very brightest, to piece together the patchwork of subjects into a coherent pattern of understanding. It is this more than anything else which leads to the divorce between learning and life in academic schools, and to the futile aim of learning for learning's sake. Learning gets its vitality from its relationship to life. Learning that has no roots in continuing experience soon gets forgotten. What we don't use we lose. Traditional secondary education ignores these facts. It also cuts off young people from understanding the interdependent nature of things, which is an essential quality of mind in the modern world.

Another educational anomaly arising from the academic illusion is that, quite often, the less academic children are given courses of a broad, integrated kind, with plenty of relevance to life, while those being hand-polished for high examination attainment are denied a proper preparation for personal and civic life, even though they have the vote at eighteen and will, presumably, be destined for leading roles in the management of society. We shall look into this further in Chapter Six.

Mercifully the academic illusion is no longer as influential as it once was. There is much talk of broadening curricula and relating subjects to one another and to life. Some valuable changes have already been made by innovative schools and Examining Boards. Even so, the dead weight of the learn-it-regurgitate-it process of academic education, with its once-for-all examination goal, or series of goals, impedes the very growth and expansion which could revitalize the secondary school curriculum. The heroic efforts on the part of the teachers to incorporate exciting and challenging 'General Studies' into the curriculum of the able students may be largely wasted because the students themselves, by now deeply imbued with the idea that education is not about personal development but about passing exams, denigrate General Studies as not worth bothering about. This can be offset by making General Studies compulsory for school-leaving and university entrance examinations, which is the situation in some parts of the world. But the risk of compulsion is that General Studies itself may be killed by the academic approach and become yet another memory load instead of a liberating experience.

The lack of balance in education, arising from the dominance of academic values, is well illustrated by the consideration of a common curriculum made by a Working Party of H.M. Inspectorate and published in December, 1977 as '*Curriculum 11–16*'. The Working Paper states: 'We see the curriculum to be concerned with introducing pupils during the period of compulsory schooling to certain essential "areas of experience". They are listed below in alphabetical order so that no other order of importance may be inferred: in our view they are equally important:

The aesthetic and creative
The ethical
The linguistic
The mathematical
The physical
The scientific
The social and political
The spiritual

The list is not, or should not be, surprising; but the existing curricula of many pupils might well not measure up to it very satisfactorily. It does not in itself constitute an actual curricular programme. It is a check list, one of many possible ones, for curricular analysis and construction.'

The crux of this statement is the comment 'in our view they are equally important', since, in the education of the most promising examination candidates, the linguistic, the mathematical and the scientific get the bulk of attention while the aesthetic/creative, the ethical, the social/political and the spiritual are starved of time and concern. The much-vaunted standards of the academic schools are not high at all if our yardstick is all-round human development.

How far able young people are actually damaged by an excess of academic education is a moot point, but damage certainly does occur. Dr Anthony Storr, who teaches psychotherapy at Oxford University, stated in a broadcast, published in *The Listener* for 2nd November, 1978: 'We get plenty of examples of what I now call "the Oxford neurosis", which is intellectual precocity combined with emotional immaturity.' And again, in *Youth and the Social Order*, Dr F. Musgrove makes out a good case that the academic grind impedes maturation.

Why, then, is the academic illusion still allowed to dominate so much of secondary education? The reason given is that parents and employers want certified attainments, therefore the present system must go on. This answer, of course, begs the question. There are other ways of assessing ability than by the fight against the clock in the examination hall. Moreover, the supposition itself is false. Parents may *think* that employers are solely interested in the academically trained mind but, in fact, this is not so. Employers naturally want literacy and numeracy; after that, what they most value are general competence and qualities of personality – fit minds rather than stuffed heads. In answer to questions from members of the World Education Fellowship conference held at Eastern Michigan University in the summer of 1978, the education spokesman for Fords at Detroit said: 'We don't want people whose abilities are tied down to narrow skills. We want people who are flexible and can learn.' Similar statements have been made by other leading industrialists such as Sir David Orr, Chairman of Unilever, and Mr A. A. Jarratt, Chairman of Reed International, who states: 'The prime purpose of education is to prepare the individual for life by (a) teaching those rudimentary needs which must be the basis for practical living, (b) creating an awareness in each individual of his, or her, abilities and (c) instilling a desire to utilize those abilities to the full for the purpose of self enrichment. It should be a beginning, a questioning, and an open-ended process. I certainly do not believe that its prime purpose is to serve a particular need other than that of the individual. It is the individual's needs that should be paramount and I am conscious that this is an extremely difficult objective to fulfil in an increasingly complex society where mass production, mass thinking and mass hysteria are all too common.'

The Confederation of British Industries in its Education and Training Bulletin of August 1973 shows that leading employers are just as concerned as modern educators to explore alternatives to academic examinations: 'The possibility of a profile system interpreted in its widest sense to include continuous assessment, and to facilitate the provision of a record to prospective employers, of all aspects of a pupil's personality, achievements, aptitudes and development, should be considered further.'

A particularly damning indictment of the intellectually numbing effect of too much narrow specialization came from Mr Oscar Hahn, Chairman of the awards committee of the first National Engineering Scholarships which sat in October, 1978. Only 62 scholarships were awarded out of the expected 100 because candidates were excluded who had been as he put it, 'trained like puppy dogs to pass exams'. In a recent lecture, Sir Herman Bondi pointed out that what is needed in industry and science is more imagination. He commented: 'Lack of imagination is the great brake on progress'. Even the universities, whose entry demands sustain the academic illusion, are themselves playing a double game. They require examination results as the condition of entry and then give interviews at which the main focus of inquiry is not 'How much do you know?' but 'What kind of a person are you?', although the universities' own demands impose a narrow curriculum and a load of homework on young people which curtails time for private reading and personal development.

The argument is not, of course, against intensity and depth of study as such. We should let the academically minded be as academic as they wish as long as we encourage them to develop themselves broadly as well, and give them opportunities to do so. When concentrated study is a student's road to personal fulfilment then he, or she, should be given every help to travel it – but not with such hypnotized adulation that other ways of fulfilment are made to seem inferior by comparison. What is wrong is that academic values and competitiveness have run wild in education and that many in the education industry have a vested interest in keeping it that way.

Dr W. D. Wall, Emeritus Professor of the Psychology of Education at the London University Institute of Education, makes the case for a sense of proportion about academic education in *Constructive Education For Adolescents* (UNESCO and Harrap, 1977): 'There certainly is a group of highly intelligent adolescents for whom scholarship, in its stringent sense, provided it is neither narrow nor arid, is the most valuable form of education. In the early years however, and up to the age of 14 or 15 or even older, it is doubtful whether the emphasis should be as exclusively upon memory and verbalization as is usual, or upon standards which only the ablest of a generally able group can attain in a reasonable period of time. Nor does the fact that many able adolescents do well after an intensively academic education prove such an education to be the best they might have had. The one-sidedness and even creative sterility of many intellectuals (to say nothing of their tendency towards obsessional neurosis) is in part an indictment of the kind of education they have received.'

We have reached the stage when more and more people have come to see the educational flaws in the academic illusion. Yet the grip of the academic tradition persists. This is damaging to some of the most able students and disastrous to the least able. The educational system of a democracy should be just, humane, efficient and, above all, concerned with individual development – the nourishment of personal potential. This is what our young people need – and what the future needs. It is not what at present exists. Hence the importance of courageous, fundamental change. The clear, unequivocal message is that the academic illusion must be replaced by the application of developmental principles to what we teach, the way we teach, the context of learning, and how we assess the learning process. The time has come to stop the sacrifice of young minds to the academic gods. In the next chapter we shall consider an unexpected confirmation of this in recent findings from the study of brain physiology.

4

HOBBLED MINDS

The secondary school system, as we have already noted, is not, and never has been, based on scientific principles. Why, for example, have we tended to teach most subjects in forty or forty-five minute chunks? There is no scientific justification for this whatsoever; indeed, it is, psychologically, inefficient. Why x periods a day and y weeks in a term? Just habit and tradition. Why have homework? The homework load varies hugely from one school to another, and yet all schools are ostensibly pursuing the same objectives. What is the optimum homework-time in terms of desired attainment? Nobody knows. In general, the essential research has not been done.

We are, then, short on principles by which to make the reforms of secondary education for which everyone is asking. Fortunately, the physiologists have now come up with something firm for us to take hold of. This is the discovery that the two hemispheres of the human cerebral cortex have different functions and require different educational approaches. That does not solve all our problems for us, but it is a valuable starting point. We shall have to go into this in some detail as the facts are not as widely known among educators as they should be.

To make the position clear, we must digress briefly into how we have come to acquire the knowledge now at our disposal. The story begins in the last century when the French physician, Paul Broca, discovered that the speech centres of man are located in one hemisphere only – usually the left. As speech is so central to personal and social life, the left hemisphere of the cortex came to be considered the dominant hemisphere, the right one being relegated to a minor role of an unspecified kind. We now know that the cortex is not a dominant-and-subsidiary system but a partnership of two brains, each endowed with its own special functions, and that the two together are beautifully equipped to complement each other's roles in helping man to comprehend his environment and act effectively upon it. In addition to their differentiated functions, the two hemispheres share some components of mental life – memory for example.

This dramatic discovery about our brains has come upon us rather suddenly as the result of a number of streams of research coalescing since World War II in a way which has greatly extended our understanding of the incredible organ that lies between our necks and the crowns of our heads. The war itself was one factor. During the war, on the Russian front in particular, every conceivable non-fatal injury to the brain occurred, leading to careful study and treatment. This helped to reveal the differences in capability that resulted from left or right hemisphere injuries.

A second stream of information came from an entirely unexpected source. A team of surgeons in the United States became involved in an attempt to help, by surgery, acute epilepsy that had failed to respond to any other treatment. Epilepsy is a minor or major neural explosion which starts at a focal point in the brain and spreads into surrounding areas, with symptoms that vary according to its intensity. The two hemispheres of the cortex, which lie like half caps at the top of the brain on either side of the midline, are independent of each other except for a nerve mass, called the *corpus callosum*, which permits neural communication between the hemispheres. The surgeons reasoned that if they severed the *corpus callosum* this would insulate one hemisphere from the other and so prevent the epileptic disturbance from affecting the whole brain. The operation was carried out and had some success in relieving acute incapacity caused by epilepsy. At first, to everyone's surprise, there seemed to be no side effects, but more stringent investigations revealed startling differences in the way each half-cortex responded to stimuli. It was found, for example, that the

28

left hemisphere was adept at handling words but not patterns, and that the right hemisphere was good at recognizing and recalling patterns but was, virtually, dumb. Other knowledge of the two hemispheres came from fixing electrodes to the scalp and then seeing how the hemispheres 'light up' with activity when subjects are given varying things to do, such as listening to music or doing sums.

A further source of information came as the result of a change in technique when giving electric shock therapy to relieve people suffering from acute neurotic symptoms. The treatment was found to be less disturbing to patients when administered alternately to the two sides of the brain. Since such shocks temporarily depress brain activity, the treatment offered an additional opportunity to study the specific functions of each hemisphere independently. Once again, remarkable differences in response were found. Of course, we are not, as it were, two people in one head, but we do have a bi-modal consciousness.

The pattern that emerges from these various researches is not a precise dichotomy of function between the two hemispheres, as individual variations are found. Nevertheless, two different modes of consciousness have been established and these are, predominantly, located in the left and right hemispheres respectively. Each mode has its own special qualities and both modes require careful development and exercise through education.

The relevance for education of the new insights is noted in a report by the eminent Russian neurophysiologist, Vadim Lvovich Deglin, which appeared in the UNESCO *Courier* for January, 1976: 'One of the specific characteristics of the human brain is what is known as the functional specialization of its two sides, the left and right cerebral hemispheres. It has been discovered in the last few years that the left hemisphere of the brain controls logical and abstract thinking, whereas the right controls concrete and imaginal thinking. The personality, and modes of perception of an individual, depend on which of his two cerebral hemispheres is more developed, whether as a result of inherited characteristics *or of education*.' (Author's italics)

Overall, the work to date indicates that the left hemisphere of the cortex specializes in linguistic, logical, analytical, abstract, convergent and sequential functions; and the right in intuitional, synthetic, creative, relational, divergent and spatial functions. Now we know this, we can well understand, with hindsight, how, in the course of evolution, these contrasting but complementary functions needed special neural provision in order to process information from the environment and permit appropriate action. Suppose we consider, for example, the long era when the human species lived by hunting and food-gathering. Before a hunt, a great deal of itemized, sequential preparation and planning would be necessary. When the hunt was on, however, the skill most needed to survive, let alone succeed, would be the ability to sum up the changing situation as a totality and act with swift intuitive responses. Intuitive insight is required in all changing situations, including personal relationships.

People striving for survival in the concrete jungle likewise need a well-developed capacity for both sorts of response in order to deal with life. Indeed, *any* situation calls for a balanced response, with each hemisphere making its appropriate contribution. If Mr Jones meets Mrs Robinson in the High Street, he knows he has met her because his right hemisphere recognizes the *gestalt* of her form and movements, and he knows her name – presuming he can recall it – because his left hemisphere supplies him with the words. Another example of balanced functioning is speech itself. The left hemisphere provides the words in their meaningful order while the right hemisphere supplies the tone and rhythm. In research, as Jerome Bruner has pointed out, 'it takes a hunch to figure out first where the analytical tools should be applied.' An academic education that lacks training of the intuitive function is, consequently, only half an education. The significance of the harmonious functioning of both hemispheres cannot be over-emphasized. Professor Robert Ornstein writes in *The Psychology of Consciousness*: 'The polarity and the integration of these two modes of consciousness, the complementary workings of the intellect and intuition, underlie our highest achievements.' Dr Roger

Sperry, one of those concerned with the original research, comments on the implications for education and society of the new discoveries in *The Psychophysiology of Thinking*: 'The main thing to emerge from the (foregoing) facts is that there appear to be two modes of thinking, verbal and non-verbal, represented rather separately in left and right hemispheres respectively, and that our educational system, as well as science in general, tends to neglect the non-verbal form of the intellect. What it comes down to is that modern society discriminates against the right hemisphere.'

This recent knowledge of brain functioning calls for a more synthetic approach to education. Dr Robert D. Nebes of the Department of Psychiatry at the Duke University Medical Center writes: 'Perhaps, when people speculate about an inverse relationship between scholastic achievements and creativity they are really talking about the effect of overtraining for verbal skills at the expense of non-verbal capacities. Many problems can be solved either by analysis or synthesis; but if people are taught habitually to examine only one approach, their ability to choose the most effective and efficient answer is diminished.'

Education of right-hemisphere consciousness includes activities and experiences which synthesize knowledge, organize perceptions in patterns, relate things together, are concerned with tone, rhythm, the apprehension of beauty, immediate sensuous awareness, visualization, imagination, metaphor, creativity, spontaneity, and intuition. Right hemisphere consciousness looks round corners; orientates spatially; takes pleasure in form and wholeness, responds to totalities. It is the obverse as well as the complement of the analyzing, verbalizing, logical activities which characterize the education of the left-hemisphere style of consciousness. A complete education should develop right and left hemispheres equally.

Untold damage has been done in the past, and is still being done in the present, by disregard for the right-hemisphere functions of the mind. Early intelligence tests were heavily biased on the linguistic-mathematical side so that millions of children with high right-hemisphere skills must, over the years, have found themselves rejected by IQ selection, at great cost both to themselves and to society. And all along the line, secondary schools and universities have directed most of their attention to the development of the left hemisphere functions. It is like training a person for a race by constantly exercising one leg while leaving the muscles of the other leg to atrophy. Reviewing the situation from the point of view of a neurosurgeon, Dr Joseph E. Bogen writes in *The Human Brain*, 'It means that the entire student body is being educated lopsidedly.' The modern concept of a cultivated mind is that of one capable of well-balanced, bi-modal apprehension and response.

These discoveries about our brains give a fascinating fresh slant to the history of education and psychology. The great innovators in the education of the adolescent, Decroly, Neill of Summerhill, Curry of Dartington, Badley of Bedales, John Dewey, Jerome Bruner and others have all moved educational practice on from the narrow to the broad, from excluding feeling to including it, from passive receptivity to active participation, from direction to spontaneity, from copying to creating, from the impersonal to the relational, from the academic to the human, from the isolated to the social. Their intuitions, it turns out, were well-founded. They sensed the omission of something vital in the education of adolescents and set out to remedy it. What they felt to be lacking, we now see, was, for the most part, the proper education of the right-hemisphere functions.

Psychology has a similar story to tell. Psychologist after psychologist has drawn attention to the bi-modal aspect of human consciousness. Pavlov came to the conclusion that humanity could be broadly divided into two types: the artists and the thinkers. William James wrote of the tough-minded and the tender-minded, and Jung of introverts and extraverts. More recently, Liam Hudson has researched into convergent and divergent styles of intelligence, R. Cohen has contrasted analytic and relational thinkers, de Bono has given us linear and lateral thinkers, and so forth. What these writers have been picking up is the natural bi-modality of the human mind. Their intuitive insights, like those of the educational innovators, have now been scientifically confirmed.

The outcome of all this is not that humanity is divided into two species but that every person is a combination of left and right hemisphere functioning. The psychologists named above spotted that some of us are left-hemisphere dominants while others are right-hemisphere dominants. When we add to this that the secondary system of education has obviously been designed by left-hemisphere dominants for left-hemisphere dominants, we at once see one reason why a considerable number of young people do not fit into it at all well. An adolescent who is a right-hemisphere dominant will feel miserable in, and alienated from, a school that has a strong left-hemisphere bias – as most schools have.

Dr Michael Gazzaniga, a psychologist of the State University of New York, sums up the likely situation for a child who is a right-hemisphere dominant: 'When a child's talents lie in visual-spatial relations and he, or she, is being forced into a curriculum that emphasizes the verbal, articulatory modes of solving a conceptual problem, this child will encounter enormous frustration and difficulty which may well result in hostility toward the teacher and, worse, toward the learning process itself.'

Many adults too have been led to undervalue their powers because their strengths lie in right-hemisphere functions, which they have been taught to regard as inferior.

Teachers also suffer from the excessive adulation in many schools of the left-hemisphere functions. Art teachers, Music teachers, teachers of Drama or Movement and Social Studies teachers may find themselves assessed as educational lightweights as compared with the solid worth of the Maths and Physics specialists. In fact, the education of synthesis, imagination and the creative impulse is at the core of subjective education, without which objective education lacks depth and form, leaving us, as Matthew Arnold put it, 'with overtaxed heads and palsied hearts'. Herbert Read made the case for this nearly forty years ago in *Education Through Art* and it has been taken further in such books as Witkin's *The Intelligence of Feeling* and Ross's *The Creative Arts*, but

Arts teachers, and others concerned with synthesis still have to battle against the attitude that what they have on offer is a soft option, a frill to the real business of education. They may seriously jeopardize their chances of professional advance by specializing in right-hemisphere attainments. Headships rarely come their way.

Relevant here is the interesting issue of how the education of feeling is related to the different functions of the two hemispheres. The development of feeling in personality, through formative experience, is still an elusive area for psychologist and educator. Both hemispheres have feed-back systems with the mid-brain where emotional impulses are processed or generated. Of the two hemispheres, the right would seem to be more involved with the development and refinement of feeling since one of its tasks is to mediate sensuous experience – the impact of the world on the senses.

The phenomenon of the 'late developer' may be explicable in terms of hemisphere dominance. A child with high right-hemisphere capabilities may have difficulties in finding any way to take off in a school that undervalues his powers – Winston Churchill appears to have been one of these. Similarly, a natural left-hemisphere personality, who is hungry for academic challenge, may be thwarted and irritated in classes that are trying to be broad but are, in fact, failing to offer any intellectual challenge. A balance in which all children can feel at home is what every school should seek to be. Anything other than that is going to exclude and discourage. Through lack of total mobilization a mind may never get out of bottom gear.

The concept of bi-modal education exposes a serious weakness of traditional secondary education which has not so far been mentioned – the tendency to build on strength and to neglect weakness. Students are encouraged to concentrate on what they are good at and to drop what they have no flair for. Up to a point this is sensible, and follows the student's own inclinations. The trouble comes when academic success is the sole criterion of choice by teacher and student so that both collude in narrowing down educational experience until it becomes hopelessly inadequate as preparation for life. The proper climate for education is not that it is wise to neglect weakness in favour of strength but that it is often more rewarding to do something badly than not to do it at all, i.e; that it can be fun trying. Schooldays are the times when as many growing points as possible should be sown in the mind. No one can predict what will be useful and fulfilling in adult life. Hence, care should be taken to bring out the right hemisphere potentialities in left hemisphere dominants and vice-versa. Young people should be able to find their way around in both worlds of the mind. To leave them one-sided or, even, to encourage them to be one-sided – which is what the academic illusion achieves – is to impede their capacity for relationships with the environment and for enjoying life.

Excessive educational attention to left hemisphere functions has serious social consequences, apart from the mis-education, and discouragement, of many young people. So much that is lifeless, grey and cruel in society derives from our failure to educate properly the right hemisphere functions of those who control our lives. The narrow bureaucrat who sees people as items in some schedule or other, the planners who treat people as objects, the mechanistic thinkers, the 'expert' who lays down confident opinions that are nothing but the logical conclusions of a one-track mind, the civil servant busy composing incomprehensible instructions, the committee member who thinks everything is solved once you get the words right are all victims of an educational system that has overtrained the intellectual, logical functions and neglected the development of intuition, synthetic thought and immediate apprehension of the real situation. Such people resent and resist change and, as administrators, prefer 'No' to 'Yes'. They live incarcerated in a set of concepts and theories that 'ought' to work, and are ill-equipped to understand why they do not. They interpret the robust tendency of actual people not to conform to standardized expectations as an irritating frailty of the human species, not as evidence of interesting breadth and variation.

Neglect of the subjective, intuitive, aspects of education has contributed to the current widespread rejection of

35

science. The young experience the lack of balance as 'being processed' and many distrust science as too objective to be human. This creates a dangerous schism in our technological culture. In *The Nature of Human Consciousness* Dr Thomas Blackburn writes: 'The salient feature of the counter-culture is its epistemology of direct sensuous experience, subjectivity, and respect for intuition – especially intuitive knowledge based on a "naive" openness to nature and to other people. Both on its own merits and as a reaction to the abuses of technology the movement has attracted increasing numbers of intelligent and creative students and professional people. I believe that science as a creative endeavour cannot survive the loss of these people; nor, without them, can science contribute to the solution of the staggering social and ecological problems that we face.' He adds: 'It seems to me, however, that some undeniably dangerous attitudes do exist in science's present stance towards nature; and, to the extent that these attitudes exist, they represent dangers to the integrity of human freedom and the terrestrial environment.'

The attitudes in question are those which result in analysis without synthesis, in abstractions without studying the relationships between abstractions, in exploiting natural resources without taking proper account of the consequences for people. All these are sicknesses resulting from the atrophy of right-hemisphere consciousness. They account for the anti-intellectual movement of our times. The way to counteract this unfortunate development is to bring a proper bimodal balance into education. No educational system can possibly be rated as adequate if it fails to nourish and exercise the whole brain.

Some schools and teachers are trying to offset the isolation of the intellect in education and the consequences of that isolation, but there are still too few of them. Nor are they as yet sufficiently aware that they are not only educationally right, and humanly right, but that they have brain physiology on their side. This new knowledge should quickly correct the academic illusion and the lop-sided education it produces. But will it? Not without a struggle. There is too much ego-investment among the high priests of the specialist domains for them to yield readily to the tide of opinion and knowledge mounting against them.

A study of differential brain functioning calls for a transformation of both the content and process of education. In the next chapter we shall consider one aspect of this – the education of personal competence.

GUIDE TO THE HEMISPHERES
(items drawn from various studies)

LEFT MODE OF INTERACTION WITH THE ENVIRONMENT	RIGHT MODE OF INTERACTION WITH THE ENVIRONMENT
Logic	Intuition
Analysis	Synthesis
Objective	Subjective
Intellectual	Sensuous
Rational	Metaphoric
Propositional	Imaginative
Verbal	Spatial
Abstract	Concrete
Reductionist	Compositionist
Sequential	Simultaneous
Differentiating	Integrating
Convergent	Divergent

A glance at these lists immediately shows the undue emphasis on left hemisphere functions in the traditional style of secondary education.

SOME DIMENSIONS OF HUMAN COMPETENCE

Personal competence is a highly prized human attribute. It is vital to individuals and to society. And yet we hear very little about this quality in secondary education, which is, overall, much more concerned with teaching and using facts than with the art of living. This is yet another spin-off from the academic illusion which makes learning, remembering, reasoning, and reproducing knowledge seem to be much more important than feeling, being and doing. Where, then, do adolescents learn to be capable as persons, if and when they do learn it?

Some case histories may help to answer the question of how the young acquire competence as human beings and, incidentally, to reveal the nature of the gap between institutionalized learning and individual lives within the secondary system. Michael is attending a comprehensive school which everyone considers to be a good one. It has an enthusiastic head teacher, a carefully-designed curriculum, a competent staff, and facilities that are well up to standard. The snag, so far as Michael is concerned, is that he does not find himself fitting in well. The reason for this is that Michael is what John Holt calls a 'do-er'. He has a mind of his own and knows what he wants from life and how he intends to go about it. Unfortunately, his plans for himself do not coincide with the school's plans for him. He has committed the unforgivable sin of refusing to accommodate himself willingly to the combination of choices which the curriculum has on offer. He accepts some of it as important to *his* life, while rejecting what he feels to be irrelevant. His technique of rejection is simply not to do what he does not see as being of value to him. This self-determination falls right outside the school's range of tolerance. The teachers accuse Michael of wasting their time and being uncooperative.

Michael's private life contrasts sharply with his school life. He is always busy with one or another of his interests. At fourteen he is so well-versed – self-taught at that – in the intricacies of motor vehicles and other equipment that he is in constant demand for repairing friends' mopeds, cars and other pieces of machinery. In this he has a reputation for both skill and reliability. Over the week-ends – and illegally as it happens, because of his age – he is acting as assistant chef at one of the local restaurants. He can put on a faultless meal – drinks to dessert – and can make a wedding cake to professional standards. He is, in fact, an extremely capable person. But his school can find no way of exercizing Michael's capabilities in a way that is satisfying to him. And this at a time when the nation is seriously short of engineers.

Roger poses broader problems. A very able son of intelligent, cultured parents, he dropped out from school only weeks before he was due to take his qualifying examinations for university. His comment was: 'They were all waiting to chalk up my results so I thought I would give them a surprise.' He did. His school was horrified; his parents outraged. Roger went overseas, earning his living by a variety of casual jobs – lorry driver, carrier, milkman and so forth. He married a rather inadequate young woman of whom his parents completely disapproved and set about exploring life and gaining experience. The marriage broke up. Casual work began to pall. Looking around for something more demanding, Roger found himself fascinated by what was happening in the computer world and applied for a training course. He was accepted, presumably on personal interview, as his academic qualifications were thin. He romped through the course, was taken on by an electronics firm and is now one of the new generation of tele-processing engineers with the world at his feet.

Suppose Roger had stayed on at school, taken his examinations and gone to university, would he now be more or less competent as a human being, more or less well set-up for a successful life? During his years out in the world, he has learnt self-reliance, initiative, human sensitivity, how to manage himself and others in the give-and-take of real encounter, how to handle money and the intricacies of bureaucracy, and he has gained a perspective on opportunities which has enabled him to select a field of work which, at any rate for the present, he finds absorbing and fulfilling. The immediate response of anyone who meets Roger now is, 'What a delightful and intelligent young man!' He is totally transformed from the edgy, rather inaudible and somewhat hostile seventeen-year-old who walked out of the academic obstacle race.

Many university students are also delightful and intelligent but there are a number of them who are uncertain and insecure, as we see in Dr Anthony Storr's comments on 'the Oxford neurosis' quoted earlier. And what are we to make of the brilliant young linguist who visited the student counsellor because, although he could recite love poetry in four languages, he was too shy to carry on a conversation with a girl in any of them? An educated person? What exactly had happened to his education for social competence?

Tim's experience is somewhat different again. He followed the *cursus honorum* through to a Ph.D. but in rather unusual circumstances. He was a slow developer and came to his secondary school as a late entrant. The specialist teachers were careful to warn him that he would have to concentrate exclusively on his studies if he wanted to reach examination standard. Tim, however, had other ideas. He was interested in radio apparatus, and Hi-Fi – electronics generally – and also photography. In spite of complaints to the headmaster from the specialist staff, he refused to drop his personal interests. In the end, he did well enough academically to get to university, where he studied psychology. The combination of psychology, electronics and photography equipped him for specialist research into pilot fatigue, instrument panel design and other problems, in which he was so successful that, after holding a top position in the U.K., he was tempted away from Britain by the 'brain drain'.

What exactly accounted for Tim's attainments? His school or his own strength of mind? Obviously, his school made a contribution to his ultimate achievement, but supposing he had narrowed himself down as his teachers wanted? Tim, incidentally, was a typical right-hemisphere personality: broad, imaginative, fond of poetry and music, and good at synthesizing different things together in order to solve specific problems.

The case of Vera gives yet another slant on the possible gap between what a school teaches and competences needed for life. I met Vera first as a part-time secretary who did some work for me. Shortly afterwards I discovered that she had five children, although she was still only in her early twenties, and that she was separated from her husband, whom she had married when she was seventeen. The children were boarded out temporarily and the problem was to find a house for Vera and her family. That achieved, she settled down with good humour and competence to look after her children, run the home, and take in odd consignments of typing. She was, in fact, a thoroughly capable young woman.

One day when I dropped by with some typing, I noticed that Vera's second youngest was playing with a school exercise book. When he had finished with it, I picked it up and found it was Vera's geography exercise book from her schooldays. She had not been in the examination stream, but the book was immaculately kept, with plenty of facts about various parts of the world, accompanied by neat, coloured maps. I asked Vera if I might ask her some questions from the book. She agreed, and I did. So far as I could make out, no information from her geography lessons had survived. As India and Australia were prominently featured in the exercise book, I concluded by asking what direction a ship would take if it was travelling from India to Australia. She had no idea. Apparently two periods a week of geography for fifteen terms had left no observable traces. The actual skills she was using in running her home she had

41

learnt mainly from her mother. Her typing came from secretarial college. Apart from the basics, what did school teach her that had a follow-through into her life?

There were certainly some things that it *could* have taught which *would* have been of use to her in later years. One thing she very much needed, as she had a man friend, was accurate knowledge of birth control. There had been some sex education at her school but nothing on contraception. As she did not read books or women's magazines, what she knew of contraception she had picked up from playground gossip so that she had come to think of the whole thing as 'rather nasty'. It took two more children and a kindly general practitioner to get her to change her mind. Nor, at school, had she been taught about insurance or Social Security or filling up forms, or the law, in all of which she became caught up as a young married woman with responsibilities for home and children, and whose absent husband was dodging maintenance payments. Or again, Vera, in spite of her high general competence, got into difficulties with her budget, through sheer ignorance, when she was duped and dazzled by the dubious arithmetic of door-to-door salesmen into purchasing by instalments some needed items for the home. That sort of thing had *not* come into her arithmetic at school.

Sandra was a more independent girl. She matured early, detested school, and, by the time she was 15, spent her evenings with friends exploring life instead of doing her homework. This led to a collision with her parents who would have liked her to qualify for university. After a disastrous two years she left school but had no difficulty in finding work as she was personable and competent.

Such cases open up the whole matter of what human competence is and how it is acquired. We can be reasonably sure of two things. Personal competence is unlikely to be educated by too much tutelage and by too much spoon-feeding of the mind. Competence is more likely to grow in a context which combines freedom to develop, encouragement to think for yourself, and commitment to what is felt *personally* to be significant. As things are, therefore, secondary education does little to help adolescents to develop competence in life. It persistently dodges this important educational trust.

When we extend our perspective to include the whole of society, failure to educate for personal competence is frighteningly obvious. Three-quarters of the people in prison are not so much criminals as inadequate personalities. Then we have the alcoholics, the broken marriages, the ineffective parents, the chronic neurotics and hosts of dependent personalities – all showing the marks of poor personal development. The schools are not, of course, exclusively responsible for this sad human flotsam and jetsam. The homes and society too are heavily implicated. But the schools must accept a considerable part of the responsibility if they do not give personal development a high priority – which most of them do not.

If we are to get anywhere with educating competence, it is necessary to arrive at some conclusions about what are the elements of human competence, as distinct from specific technical skills. No doubt different people would list different components. By way of a start, perhaps the following three groups of components would receive fairly general acceptance:

THE ABILITY:

to communicate thoughts and feelings by speech and writing

to handle numbers, money and mensuration in real-life situations

I. Basic Personal Competence

to evaluate statistical statements on everyday issues, and to understand the meaning of probability and 'average'

to read fluently

to earn one's own living

to be able to entertain oneself

This is familiar ground educationally but calls for one or two comments nevertheless. Standards of spoken English are often given little attention in schools. It is a curious sort of education that does not provide adolescents with the ability to express their feelings verbally. The tumult of emotion demanding an outlet is left seething inside. To lack verbal fluency seriously inhibits effective human relationships in after life. For example, marriage guidance counsellors tell us that poor quality of communication between partners is a common element in failure of mutual adjustment. Violence, too, can be the consequence of poor verbal capacity. The fists come out when the words fail.

THE ABILITY:

to relate to others

to accept responsibility for oneself

to be sensitive to the needs and feelings of others

to think for oneself

to be able to think laterally as well as linearly

to listen to what others are saying

to reason with intelligence and feeling

II. Social Competence

to make intelligent choices between alternatives

to cooperate with others in the pursuit of common aims

to take the initiative when it is appropriate to do so

to set oneself realistic goals

to tackle complex situations

to understand and accept emotions

44

to tolerate unavoidable
frustrations

to acquire a set of principles by
which to live

No doubt this list is somewhat idealistic. It is also incomplete. Yet, thinking over the general components of social competence does give a direction to the educational process which is lacking in the traditional secondary system. It is interesting to observe that, when we make a list of this kind, whereas some of the components of competence can be developed in the ordinary classroom situation, others need the context of direct experience and action for their exercise.

III. Personal Qualities	Self-reliance Confidence Curiosity Concentration Persistence Reliability Flexibility Far-sightedness Imagination

That is a short list of qualities which are indisputably components of personal competence. They can be helped or hindered by the quality of education provided. For example, a fifteen-year-old sitting in class who is not interested in X, is not learning X but is learning to be bored and inattentive. Conversely, an adolescent who is excited by Y is learning not only Y but also concentration and possibly pertinacity, at the same as he is having his curiosity stimulated. Learning, or failing to learn, personal competence is the hidden curriculum of every lesson, every experience.

When we break down personal competence into its elements we at once see that it is a complex, high-order quality to the achievement of which the schools should direct persistent effort if they are to prepare young people for happy and effective lives. This is not only true in personal terms but in career terms also. A number of business men were asked whether, if they had to make the choice, they would rather have a secretary who spelt and typed perfectly but was rather unreliable and not very cooperative or one who was thoroughly reliable and cooperative but had to keep a dictionary on her desk, and occasionally had to retype a letter. They all gave priority to personal qualities. There is, of course, every reason to hope for secretaries who are both reliable *and* good spellers! Competence may or may not go along with academic ability. It should be educated and valued in its own right. If, within our schools, we ignore competence as an important personal attribute, those who have it, but are not scholastically inclined, may well feel undervalued and resentful, and may then turn their powers against the school and, later, the society that has failed to appreciate them.

Teachers are well aware of the importance of personal qualities but do not always act upon that knowledge, because the drive for examinations success deflects them from their educational objectives. The most comprehensive study yet made of the development of personal competence in schools has recently been completed by John Raven of the Scottish Council for Research in Education. It was published in 1977 by H. K. Lewis under the title *Education, Values and Society*. An interesting part of Raven's research was his exploration of the gap between the aspirations of teachers for the personal development of their pupils and their own assessment of how far these aspirations were achieved in the teaching of their more academic pupils. The results for non-academic pupils were much the same. The inquiry included an investigation of the percentage within a sample of 1,200 teachers who regarded the items Raven presented as 'very important'; the percentage who said they tried hard to achieve the objectives in their own lessons, and the percentage who thought themselves to be very successful or moderately successful in achieving the objectives with their pupils.

Results worked out as follows for items rated as important by over 80% of the sample of teachers.

		% of teachers who:		
	AIM	Thought aim very important	Tried hard to achieve aim	Felt very or moderately successful in achieving aim
1.	Help them to develop their characters and personalities.	93	53	49
2.	Encourage pupils to be independent and to be able to stand on their own feet.	92	53	40
3.	Make sure that they are able to read and study on their own.	92	59	41
4.	Encourage them to have sense of duty towards the community.	90	59	46
5.	Ensure that all pupils can speak well and put what they want to say into words easily.	89	55	40
6.	Encourage them to have opinions of their own.	89	60	48
7.	Help them to develop a considerate attitude towards other people.	88	63	42
8.	Help them to think out what they really want to achieve in life.	82	34	33
9.	Ensure that all students can express themselves clearly in writing.	82	57	52

47

10. Teach them about what is right and wrong.	82	57	61
11. Give them experience of taking responsibility.	81	43	44

Item 23 in Raven's list shows the conflict in teachers' minds between educating for life and educating for examination results:

	% of teachers who:		
AIM	Thought aim very important	Tried hard to achieve aim	Felt very or moderately successful in achieving aim
Help them to do as well as possible in external examinations.	68	76	83

The students show a similar duality which is, of course, imposed by the secondary system itself. They want to gain their examinations but also: 'Pupils who wanted interesting, achievement-oriented work were particularly anxious that education should provide opportunities to develop qualities of personality and character, the ability to handle responsibility, the ability to think independently and form one's own opinion, self-confidence, willingness to stand on one's own feet, and the ability to get on with others.'

The research quoted above was conducted in the Republic of Ireland but it is clear that results would be similar if inquiries were carried out elsewhere. Indeed, Raven himself supplemented the results in England and Wales. In all, the studies of Raven and his colleagues embraced 35,000 pupils, teachers and parents. What has been quoted above is only a fraction of their work.

The less able academically *may* have the advantage of a less abstract, better integrated educational experience but their chance of developing human competence at school is jeopardized by their feeling that they are second rate citizens. It is very difficult to give children a sense of self-reliance, confidence and social responsibility when the entire school structure is shouting at them that they lack what it takes to get anywhere that really matters. Raven sums up the situation as he sees it: 'The examination system, which plays such a major role in determining teacher behaviour, needs to adapt so that it can give both teachers and pupils recognition for working toward the goals which most people connected with education believe to be the most important. This examination system needs to be competency-oriented and somehow to come to terms with the fact that different pupils will have developed very different competencies with the result that it would be unreasonable to attempt to measure them all against the same, or similar, criteria or standards.'

Before leaving Raven's list, I cannot resist quoting the last item since it is so clearly shows the typical grimness of the secondary education system:

AIM	% of teachers who:		
	Thought aim very important	Tried hard to achieve aim	Felt very or moderately successful in achieving aim
Encourage them to have a good time	13	7	16

'No subject,' said Pestalozzi, 'is worth a sou if it destroys courage and joy.' The capacity to enjoy life is an important element in human competence and it is sad that teachers should rate it so low, especially now that we are facing a future in which those who cannot make use of increased leisure in rewarding self-determined activities will be the helpless victims of institutionalized entertainment.

Some schools, of course, are in tune with the need to develop personal capability. For example, one Headmistress of an 11 – 16 comprehensive girls' school, who is keenly aware of the need, believes that the experience of responsibility is crucial to personal and social competence. She explained: 'We have a wide range of responsible roles on offer from which our senior girls can select.' I asked if the girls made use of this opportunity; 'Oh yes, most of them are eager to.' One of the choices is to act as assistant tutors in the younger year groups. There are many other available roles. Unfortunately such a school is the exception rather than the rule. Dr Mia Kellmer Pringle, in her book, *The Needs of Children* includes 'The need for responsibility' among the four primary needs of children and adolescents.

What is the relationship between the content of this chapter and the last one? It lies in the fact that once we leave the narrow climate of subjects and text-books and turn instead to the development of competence for living, both hemispheres of the cortex are mobilized and exercised. Competence is dealing effectively with an immediate situation. It is more intuitive than intellectual; it is, therefore, largely a right-hemisphere response. To make a meal which looks attractive and tastes good, Michael has to weigh and measure with precision at the same time as he is coordinating a complicated cooking programme and attending to the aesthetics of his presentation. That sort of mixed functioning is what real life is about. Life, tackled in all its aspects, fully mobilizes a brain that was designed for just this sort of encounter with whole tasks. We only get an uneven exercising of the hemispheres when activities are too much abstracted from the real world. Abstraction has its place in man's ceaseless effort to understand the universe he is living in, and himself within it, but it is essentially a tool of the intellect and not intelligent living itself. It should, therefore, be given only its appropriate part in education, not a predominant role. To give proper attention to educating personal competence results in bringing education to life and rescuing it from excessive narrowness and fragmentation. Education is not a matter of passive receptivity but of purposeful interaction. How to develop personal competence through educational experience will be taken further in later chapters.

But first we have something else to attend to. So far, we have largely left aside the views of the consumers of education – the students themselves. The next chapter is devoted to a record of students' educational experiences.

6

ONE THOUSAND STUDENTS

Shortly after World War II, when there was, as today, widespread concern about the gap between schooling and life, the Association for Education in Citizenship launched a survey in England into the content of sixth-form experience – that is of students 16–18 years of age – in order to find out how much time and attention was being given at this stage to the preparation for life of young people as individuals and as responsible members of the community. The findings were reported in *Sixth-Form Citizens* (Oxford University Press, 1950). The inquiry included a questionnaire. In view of the current upsurge of renewed interest in education for life at the secondary stage, it seemed a good idea to repeat the questionnaire, as a direct exploration of how things are today and as a basis for comparison of changes that have occurred. The follow-up was begun in 1975 and was completed in 1977.

The method on both occasions has been to ask first year student teachers about their last years at school. The first question reads: 'During your last two years at school, how did you study (or receive help with) the following? Give as clearly as possible the form or extent of the study or guidance. Put 'none' where it applies. Add a comment of your own if you wish to.' There follow 29 items, covering aspects of self-understanding and orientation to life. Ten colleges of education and higher education participated in the present survey, giving a fair geographical coverage over the whole of England. More than 1,000 students filled in the questionnaire. However, some entries had to be excluded – overseas students, and two sub-samples which were too small to be representative – so that the sample analysed was reduced to 943 returns.

It has a female bias, both because women are more numerous in colleges of education, and because they seem more interested in participating in inquiries of this kind. Apart from that, the sample gives a picture of the range of student experience in the 16–18 group over a large number of schools. It enables the students themselves to make their own contribution to the continuing debate concerning the content of secondary education, its values and its aims. I shall concentrate mainly on twenty items from the first question of the questionnaire, grouped under four headings.

GENERAL PERSPECTIVE:
Astronomy, How other peoples live, World History, Philosophical ideas, Different religions.

PERSONAL DEVELOPMENT AND RELATIONSHIPS:
How the mind works, The art of clear thinking, Sex education, Family life, The art of getting along with other people.

SOCIAL ORIENTATION:
Trade Unionism, The meaning of 'democracy', Economics, The way the legal system operates, Politics.

AESTHETIC ORIENTATION:
Literary appreciation, Music, Art, Dramatic appreciation, Film appreciation.

'Astronomy' may appear to some as an odd item in the General Perspective group. It was included in the 1950 sample for two reasons: a valid contemporary outlook is not possible without a general understanding of the cosmos in which we are living, and there can be few better antidotes to blasé materialism – which even in 1950 was obtrusive – than an appreciation of the vastness and mystery of the universe as revealed by astronomy. The reasons apposite in 1950 are even more cogent today. The section 'Aesthetic Orientation' could well have included an item on the critical appreciation of television but this was not a key issue in 1950. However, large numbers of young people do still go to the cinema fairly frequently. 'Movement' should also have been included but was, unfortunately, omitted as its educational value was not then fully appreciated.

Returns on each item have been graded under three headings: 'Competently dealt with', 'Touched on' and 'None'. Any positive reference is regarded as justifying the classification 'Touched on'. The following statements, one from each section, give examples of the grading:

WORLD HISTORY

GRADING	STUDENTS' STATEMENTS
Competently dealt with	*A level course in world history from 1732.
Touched on	Occasionally discussed in General Studies.
None	None.

SEX EDUCATION

Competently dealt with	Course of lectures. Outside Lectures. Films. Books in Library.
Touched on	Very vague – embarrassed staff.
None	None throughout entire school life.

ECONOMICS

Competently dealt with	At A level.
Touched on	Very little – in history.
None	None.

ART

Competently dealt with	Taken at A level.
Touched on	A little.
None	None at all.

* 'A level' means Advanced level in the English General Certificate of Education examination.

Table II shows the twenty items broken down into the three categories and expressed as percentages rounded to whole numbers. A small proportion of 'no scores' has been omitted from the table:

Subject	Competently dealt with	Touched on	None
	%	%	%
GENERAL PERSPECTIVE			
Astronomy	2	4	92
How other peoples live	28	23	47
World History	30	16	53
Philosophical ideas	18	17	64
Different religions	31	20	48
PERSONAL DEVELOPMENT AND RELATIONSHIPS			
How the mind works	14	13	71
The art of clear thinking	9	12	78
Sex education	10	27	62
Family life	13	13	73
The art of getting along with other people	7	16	77
SOCIAL ORIENTATION			
Trade Unionism	29	18	52
The meaning of 'democracy'	28	17	54
Economics	23	15	62
The way the legal system operates	20	15	64
Politics	32	21	46
AESTHETIC ORIENTATION			
Literary appreciation	68	8	24
Music	35	14	49
Art	39	14	46
Dramatic appreciation	40	16	43
Film appreciation	10	12	77

The variation of provision for all the items is remarkable. It is also noticeable, from the comparison of individual questionnaires, that the alternative for students in many schools is all or none. For example, if a student does not take Art or Politics at A level, then these areas may be completely neglected during the last two years at school. This is confirmed from another source – the General Studies Association's Report of 1976. Its finding is that 'a planned course of general studies is *not* the norm,' Overall, by a comparison of individual returns, one is forced to the conclusion that secondary schools fall into three main types as far as general orientation to life and the broader world is concerned. There are the schools that really work at it and offer a broad and stimulating range of options; there are those that do something about it but in a rather haphazard way; and there are those that seem too busy with their specialisms to give any attention to education for life.

Nor does it seem as if much advance has been made over the past twenty-five years. If we compare the 1950 sample we get, taking the 'None' returns only, a similar picture between then and now. For example:

	1950 % (N = 296)	1975 % (N = 943)
World History	48	53
Different religions	43	48
Economics	62	62
Politics	42	46
Trade Unionism	52	52
Sex education	56	62
How the legal system operates	63	64

The two samples are not strictly comparable as they were collected in different ways, and the 1950 sample was small, but it is perhaps justified to assume that the gap in education for life in the upper reaches of the secondary school has not closed much in the past quarter of a century. The figures for sex education and politics are particularly remarkable as our young people are today having to deal with the extra challenges of the permissive society, and also have the vote at 18. Of course, nowadays, there is *more* sex education in the schools than there was, but it seems that many schools avoid the issue at the very time when young people are becoming deeply involved emotionally, may be sexually active, and are likely to be in need of discussion and information to clarify their problems. They have themselves made this plain in the present study and in others.

Again, the status of politics in the school has risen, but the general provision overall does not seem to have improved. The high proportion of 'Nones' for 'Family life' in the 1975 sample, seventy-three per cent, is in direct conflict with the widespread opinion that more should be done in schools to prepare young people for parenthood and family life. The adolescents themselves want this. John Raven, in the research already quoted, asked the boys and girls of his sample what the schools should do more of. Sixty-six per cent of boys and sixty-two per cent of girls thought the schools should 'Teach you about bringing up children, home repairs, decorating and so on', and about the same proportion wanted the schools to 'Help you to understand the implications and responsibilities of marriage.'

There have, of course, been advances in secondary education over the past twenty-five years. Secondary schools, by and large, are friendlier places, offer a wider range of subjects, give rather greater recognition – even though often still sparsely – to the expressive arts, particularly movement, drama and craft, and are more aware of the need to integrate subjects and to balance specialist study with General Studies. The good intentions are certainly there and are more widespread, but how far practice is affected in general is a moot point. The academic stranglehold remains and has not yet been weakened. Hence the tendency to regress towards the academic norm as has happened, for instance, in some Nuffield Science Projects which aimed to make science teaching more coherent and relevant to life. It is this regressive tendency which no doubt accounts for the fact that the proportion of courageous schools that struggle to offer total education, against the restricting influences of academic competitiveness, is probably no higher today than it was a quarter of a century ago.

What, one may ask, are the odds of any particular student receiving an education that is broad enough to provide a good preparation for life, as a person and as a member of society? It is extremely difficult to make an accurate assessment of this but a rough and ready pointer can be given in terms of the number of students who record *one* item as 'Competently dealt with' in *all four* of the main categories: General Perspective, Personal Development and Relationships, Social Orientation and Aesthetic Orientation. Only twenty per cent of the sample achieve this. If we apply the less stringent criterion of one item recorded as 'Competently dealt with' in *any three* of the categories, with 'Touched on' in the fourth, then the proportion reaching this standard rises to thirty-five per cent. Using this rather crude measuring rod as an indicator of whether much preparation for life is organized into senior secondary courses in England, one is left with a chance of around one in four for a particular student.

This part of the investigation also brought out contrasts that are truly astounding in view of the ostensibly common objectives of secondary education. At one extreme is the student who shows, by his or her answers, that most of the items are 'Competently dealt with', while returning 'None' for one or two, and, at the other, the student whose returns are all 'Nones', or all 'Nones' except for items that can be linked to an A level course.

There are those who hold that the sole job of the upper secondary school is to produce high academic standards, and that intelligent young people can acquire what they need of general education and preparation for life in their own time. For at least two reasons this is a fragile hope. One is the pressure of homework. The brightest and the laziest can cope with the demands by doing it at high speed or by dodging it; the conscientious students of middling ability may, and do, swot away for hours, cutting out all personal interests except at week-ends and in the holidays, which precludes continuous development and impairs social relationships and participation in community life. The other reason is the exclusive demands of the syllabus on the adolescent's intellectual life. One question in the inquiry asked 'How many books did you read during your last two years at school, apart from set books and text books on specialisms?' The results were:

I had hardly any time for additional reading	35%
I read about one book a month	43%
I read about one book a week	15%
I read more than one book a week	7%

This hardly suggests that private reading can be relied upon to put in the background to specialist education.

While the survey was in progress, concern was voiced in the press and elsewhere about the lack of provision at school for the *practical* demands of life beyond school. A question was accordingly added to test this among the students who had not as yet received the questionnaire. This sub-sample numbered 427. The question read: 'During your last two years at school were you taught about any of the following: First Aid, Keeping Healthy, Taxation, Insurance, House purchase, Careers, Social Security? Please list the ones you were taught about or write "None".' The results were as follows:

	Percentage receiving guidance
Health education	22
Taxation	19
Insurance	18
House purchase	17
Careers	65
Social security	15

Once again we see the yawning gap between learning and life.

A space was left on the last page of the questionnaire so that the respondents could make their own comments if they wished to do so. The invitation read: 'Any personal comments you would care to make on the secondary school curriculum and how you believe it should be planned in order to prepare young people for life would be much appreciated.' Half of the students in the sample took advantage of this invitation. Of those who did:

44% complained of inadequate preparation for life
26% stated that they thought the curriculum was too narrow and that there was too much specialization
24% drew attention to over-emphasis on examinations

The comments varied from a few lines to miniature essays. It is not possible to do full justice to this wealth of commentary but here are a few examples of both critical and appreciative comments.

CRITICAL COMMENTS
1. 'I have been to four secondary schools and find that all have the fault that they are exam-orientated. The curriculum is far too narrow only dealing with traditional subjects. There was a notable absence of topics such as politics, sex education, marriage, current affairs, drugs, the occult, community work, careers. Once sixth form arrived one's education was narrowed to specialising in only two or three subjects plus a general studies period of two hours.'
2. 'School should be far less a certificate factory. It should be less rigidly academic, with more work in the field of how to get a mortgage, taking or being taken to court, political ideals, multi-cultural studies, National Insurance, what to do at an interview, budgeting, economics, marriage and so on. Tolerance for our brothers too. In general, how to cope in today's world, including social problems, drugs etc.'
3. 'I think the school curriculum is geared too much towards exams, for this reason some people find they feel guilty if they read other books or pursue other interests in great detail and feel they should be getting on with the subject for which they are taking an exam. The subject a pupil likes best might not be the one in which she takes her A level, because either she isn't too good at it or they don't offer it in the syllabus – for this reason she might resent staying at school. I believe that at least once a week there should be

a short period of time set aside for the discussion of relevant topics of news, politics etc. so that the pupils do not lose contact with the outside world if, for example, they *don't* do politics, world affairs, etc. at exam level.'

4. 'My school made no attempt to prepare me (or anyone else) for life. We were very limited as regards choice of subjects and all work was very exam-oriented. In school we were not encouraged to think at all about life. As long as we remembered what the teachers taught us, we were doing OK. . . . I think it should be compulsory for secondary school pupils to learn about how other people live, law, politics and government – and even filling in forms. I don't remember the words Philosophy and Psychology being mentioned once.'

5. 'I feel that the secondary school curriculum, especially the grammar school which I attended, does not equip people for life at all. At eighteen years you can vote, but I didn't really know anything about politics. Also you need to know much more about the law and how it applies to you – my experience of wanting a divorce when I was only twenty taught me this. I would also have appreciated a wide generalised course – art, music, health, first aid, child development.'

Some returns expressed sympathy for the problems of the also-rans in the school. Here is one:

6. 'Far more emphasis should be placed on non-examination children, and not leave them to become bored and feel rejects in school. A general timetable consisting of everyday life subjects should be included in the curriculum e.g. running a home, money and how to handle it, work in the community etc.'

7. One student's comment was a single word, written in capitals: 'DESCHOOL'.

APPRECIATIVE COMMENTS

Several comments mix criticism and approval and a few are unequivocally appreciative as, for example:

1. 'My own time at secondary school was most satisfactory and I did not feel as though anything in particular was lack-

ing. There was a good balance of academic and non-academic subjects offered and choice was completely personal.'

2. 'I thoroughly enjoyed my sixth form. We worked in small groups with specialist teachers who really enjoyed their subjects. Teachers were very helpful about non-examination subjects. I was allowed to join several younger groups for subjects like needlework and woodwork. I was also allowed one morning a week doing work experience in a centre for mentally handicapped children, which I found extremely rewarding and enjoyable. I think everyone should have the chance to do some work experience, as it certainly helped me to make a definite decision career-wise.'

3. 'I was extremely satisfied with my secondary school. The academic standards were good and the teachers were efficient and co-operative. The selected syllabuses were extremely interesting and varied. Although it may appear that the school placed a great deal on academic achievement it was a very happy school and the staff were always ready to help whenever they could. Out of all my A levels I think that I enjoyed English most – it helped me to appreciate far better everything (not only poems!) in society.'

Once again we are left wondering what the odds are for John Smith to receive an education that prepares him for a full and effective personal life. We know that, today, this requires so much more than a parcel of assorted facts and limited skills; in addition it calls for flexibility of mind, breadth of understanding, aesthetic awareness, social skill, practical capability, and a lively taste for continuing education. In what proportion of secondary schools do these essentials of being a modern human being get more than perfunctory attention? The question is all the more urgent as restrictions on employment will almost certainly lead to more children staying on at school longer.

Overall, the inquiry reported in this chapter indicates that the aims of secondary schools for their senior students are unclear, that the variation of provision in education for life is extraordinarily wide, and that the chances of any student receiving a good preparation for adulthood in his or her last years at school are disturbingly poor.

So far this book has been a skirmish through the undergrowth of educational incompleteness which chokes the existing system of secondary education. We have noted disregard for the world of adolescents; obsession with academic standards at the cost of standards of individual development; blindness to the need to foster personal competence as a top priority; the tendency to treat education as end-stopped instead of being life-long; ignorance of modern brain physiology; the evidence of irrelevance to life in the typical senior curriculum; and critical reactions from the students themselves.

Faced with this perspective of cudgeled and incarcerated youth, caught up in a system of compulsion and coercion, bribe and threat, some writers, such as Paul Goodman in *Growing up Absurd*, Ivan Illich in *Deschooling Society*, and John Holt in *Instead of Education* have given up hope of reform and called for an entirely fresh start, in which education grows not from schools, subjects and tests, as at present, but from the individual drives of curiosity and search, supported by networks of learning and teaching rooted in the community itself. These critics have a case. But the schools are not going to disappear overnight, and the revolutionary changes that will transform society from what it is into the pattern they would prefer are still in the future. Meanwhile there are things that can be done at once to foster truly educational standards in our secondary schools and so make the experience of those who pass through them more formative and rewarding than is generally the case at present, while simultaneously rescuing teachers from their growing uncertainty of purpose. The rest of this book will be devoted to considering changes of method and outlook that are not only necessary but feasible as targets for the immediate future. There is, for a start, the perennial problem of what to do with the curriculum, which has been intensified by the need for a more comprehensive education of the whole personality to match our new knowledge of brain functioning.

7

CURRICULUM CONFLICT

Everyone agrees that changes are necessary in the secondary school curriculum. But what? There are plenty of views on this. Here are some of them:

There should be a good science/arts balance.
Specialist studies should be offset by breadth.
Learning should be made more relevant to life.
There should be a common core supplemented by a wide range of student options.
The curriculum should train all the modes of thinking.
The curriculum should be integrated as much as possible.
Curricula should include a creative/expressive sector.
All students should have the opportunity to acquire practical skills.
Group and individual projects should be featured.
The curriculum should provide a perspective on society and the world.
The curriculum should develop moral insight.
The development of personal competence should have a high priority.

No one would wish to quarrel with such hopes, and others like them. The problem is putting the aims into practice. How can a school do *all* the desirable things and, at the same time, meet the demands of the assessors who, wearing one hat or another, using one measuring rod or another, stand at the end of the road for most adolescents? As Professor Ronald Dore has shown in *The Diploma Disease*, the battle between education and qualification is at its height world-wide and, at present, education is not winning it.

In England, in an effort to broaden and humanize the curriculum, and to give ordinary sixteen-year-olds a chance of recognized attainment at school, the Certificate of Secondary Education (CSE) was devised which, in Mode III, gave the schools the freedom to design and assess their own curricula. That seemed very inviting and healthy, and has produced some excellent results, except that the 'recognized attainment' has *not* materialized. CSE *in toto* is regarded as inferior to the longer established General Certificate of Education. Consequently, to acquire anything less than the top grade in CSE may rank as a discredit for the individual concerned rather than a bonus. Thus, according to the National Association of Head Teachers, CSE grades 2–5 are discounted by employers as proofs of ability. This makes a sad nonsense of all the striving, since the long-laboured-for certificates turn to ashes in their owners' hands: 'For the less able pupils, who at best can only hope for low CSE grades, such examination performances sometimes serve only to increase their sense of being second-class citizens.'

At present, work is in progress in England to establish a common examination at sixteen plus which, it is hoped, will be broader and more flexible than anything we have now. Will it work out like that or will it become merely one more way of organizing educational competitiveness, with the academics acting as overlords of the system and still indifferent to what happens to personal development?

Caught between new educational purposes on the one hand, and the drive for high-status examination results on the other, what are the schools doing? Inevitably, they are compromising. By and large, the choices on offer to the students have increased, but what can teachers and pupils do but settle for unbalanced narrowness when the supreme aim put before them is to achieve the highest possible academic status through the mastery of self-contained subjects? This has the tragic effect of especially limiting the educational experience of the most able. Here, for example, is the curriculum of a bright fourth-form girl (aged fourteen) who is set on gaining a good handful of O Level results. The school runs to a 42 period cycle:

English	5 periods
Maths	5 periods
French	5 periods
Biology	5 periods
Chemistry	5 periods
Physics	5 periods
History	5 periods
Careers	1 period
Music	2 periods
Games	2 periods
P.E.	2 periods

In this curriculum, the science/arts balance is good. But what about the balance of academic to non-academic content? Excluding games and P.E. this works out at 35 : 3. There is no social or world orientation, except that which may come into history. There are no practical periods. The school concerned has practical subjects on offer – Art, Craft, Home Economics, Design etc. – but the girl has no room for them. She has chosen, in consultation with her parents and teachers, to make for the big prizes. And naturally so in the circumstances. It is the circumstances that are wrong. Notice, too, that the girl will spend a good deal of her evenings doing homework in academic subjects instead of developing her personal interests and relationships. First things – the development of the complete human being – are not being put first.

A less-academic girl in the same school is following this curriculum:

English	5 periods
Maths	5 periods
French	5 periods
Human Biology	5 periods
Needlework	5 periods
Technology	5 periods
Art/craft	5 periods
Careers	1 period

Music	2 periods
Games	2 periods
P.E.	2 periods

In this we see a much better educational balance than that in the brighter girl's curriculum. The Catch 22 of the British educational system is that if you are a high-flyer you are very likely to have a limited, unbalanced curriculum in terms of personal development, while the price that has to be paid for a well-rounded curriculum is that you end up with a low-grade, even despised, examination result, or sometimes none at all.

Limitation on education in breadth for the more able pupils is largely due to the erroneous academic conviction that separate is better. The academics want to keep their empires clearly defined so that any attempt to broaden or combine subjects is anathema to them. When integration is made – Social Studies or General Science or even 'Physics with Chemistry' – the product is immediately written off as inappropriate preparation for university studies. This motivates teachers *against* breadth and integration since, as inquiry has shown, teachers are governed in the way they organize their teaching more by questions set in earlier examinations in any subject than by the Examining Board's syllabus for that subject. Examiners are, as we all know, careful not to trespass on each other's preserves. Thus, any able student's curriculum is narrowed down, at an early stage, by the sort of questions set in the subject examinations. The minds of teachers and pupils are fettered by this.

The *crème-de-la-crème* of the British system, the Advanced Level candidates, may fare even worse than younger candidates, as we saw in the last chapter. Three or four A levels, hopefully at A, B or C grades, are a full-time occupation except for the very brightest. One bold spirit, still at school – and she is not unique – is working on Pure and Applied Maths, Physics and Chemistry. All that this leaves time for, in addition, apart from P.E. and games, is one period of Religious Education and one period of General Studies. This is no way to educate a brilliant young mind for the modern world. Another A level candidate, a boy in a school that is obviously doing its best to provide balance and breadth, is taking Spanish, French and History as his specialisms with the following supplementary courses:

Alternative Life Styles	2 periods
European Studies	2 periods
Art as a mode of lateral thinking	1 period

Incidentally, even this interesting balance is resented by some students of the school who have been for years steeped in the idea that what is not examined is a waste of time. Consequently, in an attempt to give some status to breadth, the school has decided to issue reports to parents on the five periods of general education. It is a sobering thought that numbers of highly intelligent adolescents have had their curiosity about life in the broad deadened by the methods and values of the system that is supposed to be educating them. The system is anti-educational.

Reform of the examination system for university education in England is on the way, in spite of protests from the upper echelons of secondary education. The intention is to make the examination for eighteen-year-olds broader and to include more project work and school-based work in the final assessment. But the anxiety must remain that, unless there is a fundamental change of approach at university level, in the professions, and among academics generally, the hopes for the new examination will be done to death in their turn. It is typical of the enduring academic stranglehold that, whereas the General Certificate of Education was planned as a subject examination with the specific objective of freeing the schools from the pernicious effects of the School Certificate and Matriculation examinations which preceded it, we now find ourselves rather more hog-tied than before by this 'reformed' examination system. Change itself will not rescue the adolescents from a too intense specialization; there must also be a change of heart.

This is a point where the question of maintaining high standards – so often on the lips of those devoted to the traditional style of curriculum – needs examining. What standards precisely does the traditional curriculum sustain? Certainly not standards of thinking for oneself. The message sounding down the corridors from the examination hall is not 'Think' but 'Conform'. You are allowed to think in a conventional way; *that* is approved of; but original thought is often frowned upon. John Holt feels this to be true even at university level: 'I recall talking to an old friend, then a senior at Harvard, who had enjoyed his years at college and had done very well there. I asked him whether he and his classmates very often disagreed with their professors. He laughed and said, "They (the professors) all *tell* you they want you to." But he then said he and his fellow students had learned that anyone wanting or needing an A in a course (and they all did) had better not argue with the professor. In tests, papers, even discussions, the way to get A's was to stick close to the professor's opinions, changing the language just enough so that he wouldn't think his own words were being thrown back in his face.'

This rings with the student's view quoted in the last chapter: 'As long as we remembered what the teachers taught us, we were doing OK.'

If we are to advance from the confused present to a clearer future we have to switch over from teaching subjects to teaching people. After all, what is a subject? It is an abstraction from the universal spectrum of human experience. We teach it, presumably, because it will give the person who learns it a better understanding of himself, of his environment and of his place in it; a greater capacity for living. What the curriculum should be about, then, is the development of the individual, his positive potentialities, and his competencies, and the development of understandings and relationships that enable the person to be more effective, and more responsible, in his environment – which is, today, not only the locality and the nation but the entire world. This is what subjects are about; they have no other justification whatsoever. They are nothing in themselves; they exist in the service of life or they are fictions. A subject is a door opening onto a fuller life and the real test is what the learner can find of himself and life by advancing through that door.

The problem of the curriculum can only be solved by transferring from academic to dynamic values. Of every subject we should ask what experiences, competencies and insights can be provided through it. And, of all the subjects together, we should ask how they can tie up with one another and reinforce one another. A student's curriculum should not be experienced as a lot of independent boxes piled on top of one another but as a number of overlapping circles making an intricate and exciting pattern.

This is what the concept of integration is really all about. It is a dynamic educational principle. The mind perceives, learns, remembers and thinks in patterns. The more everything is linked up with everything else the richer the mind and the more powerful the capacity for thought and understanding. All fragmentation is psychologically and developmentally undesirable. The subjects of the curriculum should be like the characters in a play, every one unique, but each interacting with the others in working through to a unified understanding of what the world is and life is. The subjects should not be like the inhabitants of a top-security jail, each locked away in isolation, giving nothing and receiving nothing from one another. Nor is it possible to give a science course balance and integration simply by the common practice of adding an arts subject to the student's curriculum, or vice-versa. This fudges the whole issue of providing a coherent pattern of learning.

Along with the purpose of integration needs to go another dynamic principle – that every subject area should carry its full educational content and not be shrunk down to the facts and processes of that particular domain. The main components of human functioning may be summarized:

The intellectual (including the intuitive)
The affective (feelings, emotions)
The social/moral
The practical/physical
The aesthetic
The creative/expressive
The spiritual (high-order functioning; 'peak' experiences)

The more of these elements – together with the components of competence mentioned in Chapter 5 – that any
educational experience can encompass, the richer and more
memorable it becomes, and the more truly formative it is.

In brief, every subject should be taught in the context of
life; this gives integration and developmental power which
is otherwise unattainable. The top point of any particular
specialism should be as high above the base as the student
can manage, but the base itself should be broad and founded
firmly in life. When all subjects are integrated within the
context of life itself, each can inform and reinforce the
others.

This can be just as true of the science specialisms, like
physics and chemistry, as it is of the humanities. Normally,
and unnecessarily, physics is limited to a narrow range of
concepts, processes and problems. It should, also, be given
its personal and social dimensions. Thus every young scientist should be encouraged to study the life of at least one
great scientist, and should be brought into encounter with
the social and moral problems created by the science in
question. A student who is being taken through the domain
of conventional physics without knowing anything of Michael
Faraday, Albert Einstein, Rutherford – to name but three
of the giants – and who has not been brought to consider,
say, the social implications of the silicon-chip revolution,
and the values of power generation and distribution, cannot
possibly be described as an educated person. Nor is he a
true scientist, by the standards of the 'Greats', if he has not
shared in the perception of the aesthetics of science, felt
wonder at the nature of things, and stirred with excitement
in the consciousness of the still undiscovered. Physics,
imaginatively taught, can reach into all those functions of
humanity listed on page 70 as well as developing general
personal competence along with competence in physics.

It is just as important that the Art student should extend
his range of apprehension to include the context of his subject. He, or she, should know what colour is, how light
functions, the derivation of pigments, the social impact and
responsibilities of Art, the comparative dimensions of the

human body, and so forth. The course should include contact with the lives of great artists, with each student, perhaps, selecting the life that he wants to study. Without the appreciation of human greatness, education is emptied of inspiration. Art, too, if broadly taught, can reach into all the functions and competencies of the human being. And so with all subjects, including mathematics which, incidentally, correlates beautifully with music. The modern Polish composer, Andrzej Panufnik, *starts* his composition with a geometrical pattern, working to and fro from diagram to keyboard until impulse and design are unified. This, incidentally, is a beautiful example of a bi-modal response to a creative task.

Broadening educational experience to include feeling and values, and perceptions that go beyond narrow subject confines, is coming to be called 'confluent education'. Dr Nasrine Adibe of Long Island University, New York, writes: 'The term confluent education is relatively new, but its philosophy can be traced down through the history of education. By reliance on common sense and insight, effective teachers have always realized that human interaction, with its full range of attitudes and feelings, is a dominant part of any instruction. Throughout the ages, such teachers have intuitively been sensitive to, and respected, the values of their students while tutoring or teaching them the knowledge and skills that had to be mastered. They have anticipated what we have come to know empirically today. Nevertheless, not all contemporary teachers are sensitive to this aspect of learning, nor have they had the patience or the know-how to deal simultaneously with the affective, cognitive and intuitive aspects of learning. Furthermore, a number of archaic views about the nature of man – his intellect, mind and body – pervasively linger on to dominate many educators' frame of reference and thus prevent them from accepting and implementing the ever-increasing knowledge of human learning.'

The academics who are, by and large, left-hemisphere dominants, in love with linear, sequential processes, and suspicious of lateral, patterned exploration and exposition, will, of course, distrust, even fear, the whole idea of confluent education, and will seek to downgrade it. But it is they who are behind the times, sticking obdurately to Newtonian formalism in a quantum age of continuous flux and flow. The education of free men in our unstable modern society *has* to be multi-faceted. In *Change and Challenge in American Education*, James Russell writes: 'The free man is aware of himself and of his environment and of the forces shaping that environment. He is aware of his own passions and of how they affect what he perceives. He knows that he perceives the world through the screen of his own personality, that the person he is colours the things he sees. He has considered his values, the values of others, and the consequences to which these values lead. He is free, in sum, not because he is without passions, but because he has examined his life and mastered it with his mind. He is a slave to no man, to no doctrine, to no ignorance. He is free because his mind has set him free.'

Informed intellectual vitality is a proper aim of education; the absorption of information alone is not. It is here that the real curriculum conflict strikes. The vaunted standards of the academics are pathetically insufficient to build up and sustain a modern man or a modern society. The qualities tested by examinations are mainly fluency in writing, a good memory, the ability to manipulate acquired processes in the solution of presented problems, and speed of working. Those four qualities are the formula for academic success. They are useful acquisitions, but they do not indicate high standards of personal development. The sort of qualities needed today, the sort of qualities needed in the future, are the qualities of personal wholeness. These are not to be attained by the traditional examination road but by the nourishment of individual uniqueness, and motivation. What this implies for education will be taken further in the next chapter.

8

TURNING THEM ON

At the heart of Britain's educational problems is a profound motivation crisis which especially affects the less able academically but also includes highly capable children who nevertheless are bored or feel that school has little to offer them. Thousands of adolescents vote with their feet every day and stay away from school on one pretext or another, with or without parental connivance. Christopher Price, in an article in the *Times Educational Supplement*, stated that 'at least ten per cent of our urban schools' are unpopular with both pupils and parents. A common complaint is that too much time is wasted in 'messing about' which is demoralizing to those who do it and infuriating to the children who really want to learn. The School Council's *Enquiry 1, Young School Leavers*, a survey of English 15 – 18 year olds published by the Government Social Survey, in 1968, showed that, of fourteen typical school subjects, only six were ranked as 'useful and interesting' by more than fifty per cent of the fifteen-year-old leavers – no great pull that, in an era when skilfully produced entertainment is constantly available in the adolescents' private lives, at the turn of a switch. Our fifteen-year-old adolescents are now at school, but are they any better motivated?

John Raven, writing about his research involving 4,000 pupils, aged 14 – 18, in the Republic of Ireland, reported in *Educational Research* for November 1977: 'About a third of the pupils sometimes or always hated going to school and felt they would be happier if they left school immediately

74

and got a job.' The National Children's Bureau Report, *Britain's Sixteen-year-olds* (1976) gives a similar proportion as being disenchanted with school. Raven writes: 'The level of disenchantment varies little with pupils' backgrounds, but it does vary with their anticipated destination in society. Forty-six per cent of those who intended to become doctors, dentists, etc. looked forward to going to school most days, compared with twenty-four per cent of those who intended to become manual workers. Fifty-one per cent of those who expected to become building and construction workers said that they would be much happier if they left school now and got a job compared with eight per cent of those who expected to become scientists.'

Raven emphasizes three points:

a. The delayed gratification hypothesis is not sustained; pupils who are going to get the best jobs *like* school; they are not delaying anything; they have their cake and eat it.

b. Those who are going to be teachers and administrators have no knowledge of what it feels like to be unhappy at school. They are unaware of the need for change.

c. The solution to the problem of school rejection seems to be more to do with running a series of courses suited to pupils who have different values and who will enter different sectors of society rather than with running enrichment programmes to adjust all to the same course.

Other research shows a relationship between being alienated from school – motivational breakdown – and actual delinquency. For example, F. J. O'Hagan of the Department of Educational Science, Notre Dame College of Education, Glasgow, reports of a recent inquiry: 'As a result of group discussions with working class pupils from areas of high delinquency it was postulated that there were at least three broad and overlapping categories of pupils attending comprehensive schools in these districts. These were termed school-orientated pupils, nonchalant pupils and anti-school pupils. An attempt was then made (by questionnaire) to ascertain some of the main differences in attitudes towards school between offenders and non-offenders. Generally speaking it was found that non-offenders occupied the first and second of the above categories and offenders the second and third.'

In other words, turn them off school and you run the risk of turning them on to crime. The possible disastrous consequence of this on a Glasgow lad is described in Jimmy Boyle's powerfully-written autobiography, *A Sense of Freedom*. He tells us: 'I never got on with any of the teachers at school and most of my pals were in the same boat. There was a void between teacher and pupil and that was it. By the age of twelve and a half there was the feeling that the teachers had given us up for lost.'

The sad point of this is that Jimmy Boyle had, as he has since proved, a tremendous potentiality. At the time he was in prison, serving a life sentence for brawling that led to a murder charge, he was invited to exhibit his sculptures at the Edinburgh Festival. He has written a play as well as *A Sense of Freedom* and is at present studying with the Open University for a degree in psychology. How, one must ask, could any school have missed such potentiality? It was discovered, in the end, as a result of the Prison Department's setting up the Barlinnie Special Unit for particularly difficult prisoners. The change of relationship with authority, and expansion of opportunities, awakened Jimmy Boyle, in a mere few months, to the realization that there were alternatives to revolt and violence. As he puts it: 'Violence is no longer my means of communication.'

Jimmy Boyle symbolizes the depressing process of betraying young people by failing to reach their real needs at school and then punishing them because their frustration explodes into violence. Spencer Millham, in his research into 1,200 young failures and delinquents, found an alarming record of rejection at school. One of the subjects complained: 'Nobody at my secondary school likes me at all.' And another: 'They're not bothered about teaching people like me.'

Look where you will in education you see waste of human powers; able pupils falling short of their optimum capabilities; ordinary youngsters driven to excesses of antagonism and revolt by a deep conviction that what the school has to offer is meaningless, and valueless to them. Teachers, from their side, are often numbed, shaken and humiliated by the blatant disregard for what they have on offer. Some leave the profession in despair; some armour themselves with cynicism; and some struggle on in a condition of depressed malaise. Others ride the storms and stay with the kids, physically and in spirit, in all kinds of difficult circumstances. Then there are those, yet again, who find themselves in pleasant schools and sail happily before the wind, rarely running into bad weather. How many of each kind of school there are nobody knows, although research is starting on this theme. The *real* facts of education, the facts below the surface statistics of attendance, exam successes and so forth, rarely *are* known.

The point is that most of the frustration and failure of adolescents, and the uncertainty and despair of teachers, could be abolished by a single, fundamental change in secondary education – founding the whole system not on the external incentives of success and failure in imposed curricula and examinations but on the actual personal motivation of the young people themselves – including their interest in future careers. The Butler Education Act of 1944 in England put upon us the responsibility for providing an education appropriate to the Age, Aptitude and Abilities of children. It omitted the most important 'A' of all – Aspirations. It is for lack of attention to the adolescents' own aspirations that secondary education falters and fails. School is only successful and satisfying for young people when what it has on offer *does* coincide with the adolescent's present interests and identification with his future. As often as not it doesn't; and that is where most of the trouble comes from. One of the male students involved in the inquiry reported in Chapter 6 comments: 'I disliked being geared to an O and A level syllabus which led to superficiality, generalities, unwanted pressure and boredom. If a pupil ever wanted to do what interested him there was no place for it at school, it had to be done at home, which meant it was ignored. My sister goes to the school I left and she is bored and would like a change from the very subjects I have suggested might

77

improve school. This seems to point out that all people have individual and highly personal requirements. Nobody is ever satisfied but it seems a great pity that people never have the opportunity to do what they would like to. After all, Education is for us and for our future, which we will one day determine.'

Developmental pyschology has now pieced together with some completeness the dynamics governing the growth of the human mind. It is this knowledge that we have to apply. To clarify the nature of the task, let us take a look at the process by which a personality emerges and thrives. We all start with a genetic hand of cards with which to play the game of life. Precisely what is there nobody knows, least of all the owner of the hand. That can be discovered only by interaction with the environment – exploration. For growth to occur, potentiality and environmental stimulus must both be present. Mozart is famous for playing the harpsichord at three years of age, and starting to compose at four. But supposing Mozart had been born in an age or society where only the crudest of musical instruments existed! Things happen, and the personality emerges, when inner potential interacts fruitfully with what exists in the environment. This is as true for the duffer as for the genius.

The human senses and brain provide the means to this formative encounter between individual and world. From the first day of life, a baby responds to the human and material environment around him; very soon he is observing it, acting upon it, trying to make some sense of it, putting together a map of his baby reality for future reference. The dynamics of this are curiosity, attention, assimilation and eagerness for experience. The return for more is the essence of the whole growth process. The happy, encouraged, self-confident child returns for more again and again; the unhappy, discouraged child, whose confidence has been eroded, hangs back or even goes into retreat. The brain has evolved to deal with the encounter with the environment and, in healthy children, it will busily get on with its job.

Piaget and his colleagues have elucidated the stages by which apprehension of the environment extends and becomes more sophisticated. When one map of the world fails to make sense of the facts of experience, it is modified in order to take in the new elements of awareness. Exactly what in the environment is perceived and made use of for personal development depends partly on what is there, partly on the genetical make-up of the child, and partly on the stimulating guidance of adults. Potentiality seeks actualization. Another factor is the impact of society as a whole. Children are inherently social beings and readily pick up what is valued and what is not in the surrounding world. This is not, however, a passive receptivity. The personal bundle of potentialities will seek fulfilment for themselves and the self-system will, in one way or another, strive to manifest its own uniqueness, hopefully in socially useful ways but, if thwarted, in some sort of useless or antisocial compensation. There is a great deal for the individual to draw on. 'We are beginning to realize,' wrote Sir Julian Huxley, 'that even the most fortunate people are living far below capacity.'

That is the barest of outlines describing some of the psychodynamics of being human. But it will serve our purpose here as long as we remember three points:

1. That the movement forward from map to map in understanding the world and interacting effectively with it is a life-long process.

2. That the process by which the individual's authentic self attains actualization is essentially personal and unique.

3. That it is only by working *with* the authentic self that we can arouse a good level of motivation.

In brief, in seeking to educate the young we must start where they are – at what R. A. Hodgkin, in *Born Curious*, calls 'the frontier' – carefully search out their potentiality for growth *as themselves* and help them along *their own path* to fulfilment as mature, though still growing, human beings. Every year should be a year of self-actualizing experience, taking the authentic personality a stage further and, simultaneously, providing the platform from which further advance may be made. If this dynamic process is distorted or destroyed by pressure to be something other than the authentic self, then the major dynamic of personal growth will be lost. Motivation and a sense of personal growth are intimately related to one another.

In practice this means that we have to individualize the secondary school curriculum. We have to start with the actual aspirations of the young people before us and not impose a curriculum on them, however carefully designed and resplendent with choices that curriculum may be. It may seem that this is an impossible aim on the grounds that the aspirations of young people will be both unrealistic and too varied to be organized in any manageable form. This is not, in fact, so. An individual's aspirations are, to a major extent, contained within the shape and style of the society in which he, or she, is living. As a rule, English boys have no great desire to become bull-fighters, while Spanish adolescents do not fancy themselves as demon bowlers. All young people growing up in a technological society can see the value in learning to read, write and calculate. They also have, or can be given, a perspective on society, and the roles they can fill in adult life. It is all going on around them. Some roles they find attractive, some not. Consequently, young people, if given a chance to do so, will be sensible about what they think they should learn, while the teacher, acting as guide in giving their aspirations realism, extends their awareness of the opportunities before them for life, work, leisure and self-development.

One headmaster of a boys' school, in an attempt to tackle the listlessness and resentment among his last year non-academics, approached them, in the term before their last year, with the invitation to say what they would like to do in their final terms at school to prepare them for their future lives. His proposal was on these lines: 'Up to now you have been following the arranged timetables. For your last year, I want you to tell us what you would like *us* to teach *you* in preparation for the life you have in mind for yourself when you leave school.' He asked the young men to talk it over with one another and with their parents, if they wished to do so, and to let him know, face-to-face or in writing, how they would like to spend their last year at school. Their requests, as it turned out, created no timetabling problems. The students were aware that they needed to build up their basic skills; there was a lot of interest in careers, and some asked for specific practical skills. Hence, their needs were met without difficulty. Where the big change came was in morale. The young men now felt that the curriculum was for them, and not something imposed from above. The headmaster checked with the group from time to time and told them: 'If anything is not working out, come and let me know.' This headmaster also gave these boys the opportunity to become 'citizens of the school' if they wished to do so. This involved taking a share of responsibility for the good running of the school. In return they were absolved from the rules affecting younger pupils. The two initiatives together cleared up the 'last year problem' which was so widespread at the time.

Leslie Smith, another headmaster, who was especially appointed to deal with a difficult situation at Mark House Secondary School, in Essex, took the principle a stage further and organized the whole of the senior curriculum on the basis of the pupils' aspirations. He gave these seniors plenty of time to think about, discuss, and express their hopes for the future. A curriculum was then framed to meet their plans for themselves. If these were unrealistic, they were gently redirected, as in this paraphrased dialogue:

BOY   I want to be an air pilot, sir.
TEACHER   Oh, yes. An interesting idea. But pilots have to know a lot of things – navigation, for instance. That means maths. How are your maths?
BOY   I'm not much good at maths, sir.
TEACHER   That's Mr Simpkins, isn't it? I'll check with him. Anyway, you are interested in aeroplanes?
BOY   Yes, sir.
TEACHER   Then if it's not possible to be a pilot, would you like to have another job at the airport – a ground job, say?
BOY   Oh yes, sir. I would, sir.
TEACHER   Then I'll check what's going, as well as having

	a word with Mr Simpkins about your maths.
	That all right?
BOY	Yes, sir.
TEACHER	Give me two or three days, then come and see
	me again. You won't forget, will you?
BOY	Oh no, sir. I won't forget. Thank you, sir.

Within two years, by building on the students' concept of their own futures, the school was converted from indolent confusion into a busy, happy place. Of course, the curriculum extended beyond career subjects but the career core, and the pupils' awareness that the school was there to help them, changed the whole climate of the school. The teachers benefitted as much as the pupils. The dreary, dead-beat feeling had disappeared. Monday morning was no longer greeted with 'Oh God – another week!'

I put to Leslie Smith the point that a lot of adolescents had no idea what they wanted to be. He felt that such a response was a cover-up, an unwillingness to share their secret world with 'the enemy'. His solution was to put the 'don't knows' on to a general curriculum while they were making up their minds. Once the school as a whole became future-oriented, the 'don't knows' tended to disappear, especially as a decision was not regarded as irrevocable, but as experimental. Other schools have also found that motivation and morale are transformed when the students' aspirations are properly respected.

Building the curriculum on pupil aspirations is especially a solution to the motivation problem for the less-academic. The academic high-fliers automatically share in selecting their own curriculum by choosing from the subject options open to them. But, even here, more could be done to personalize the curriculum. Consider, for example, the case of an able boy who wanted to take both Art and Technical Drawing at A level. He was told that he had the choice of one or the other but not both. He was passionately interested in Art, chose it, and got a good result. Now, out in the world, he wishes he had selected Technical Drawing because of the job situation.

One of the reasons for such a lack of flexibility is that schools have got into the habit of organizing themselves in year groups. Everywhere else in society, people learn wanted skills together, regardless of their ages. Schools, too, should be more prepared to organize themselves in skill and interest groups rather than in age groups. With the help of a computer, pupils and needs might then be brought to fit more snugly together.

A good level of pupil motivation is crucial for both students and teachers. This depends on increasing satisfaction while reducing frustration. We can even give this a mathematical form: $\text{Motivation} \propto \dfrac{\text{Satisfaction}}{\text{Frustration}}$
(Motivation varies as Satisfaction over Frustration).

This simple formula underlies a great deal of human behaviour. If Mr and Mrs Brown accept an invitation to spend the evening with Mr and Mrs Jones and, although the meal is good, the whole occasion is rather fraught, even boring, then the Motivation score will be low on Satisfaction and high on Frustration. In that case, the friendship is unlikely to flourish. If, however, food, conversation and companionship are well up to expectation and the only frustration is that it is an awkward place to get to, the party will break up with the feeling that 'we must all meet again soon.' The same principle applies to learning something new at any time of life. Teachers should always be considering the Satisfaction/Frustration ratio of their individual pupils, bearing in mind that whenever Frustration is considerably higher than Satisfaction, there is sure to be poor morale. It is especially important to watch this in the case of poor attainers since, having been battered so much already, their tolerance of frustration will be low. Some adolescents are being given a pounding of frustration at school which no adult would tolerate. We can hardly wonder at it if such young people are liable to rebel.

As well as future orientation, here-and-now interest is a powerful motivator. I would like to show, by reference to what happened in two schools, how such motivation can be used or wasted. The first concerns a teacher who was given a prefabricated hut and a group of young males who were rebellious academic failures. His instructions were 'Keep them quiet. There's not much else you can do.' The teacher was not so sure. After a roughish start, in which his charges made it plain they thought school a waste of time, he got them talking about motor-cycles and, the next day, came to school on his own machine and took it into the classroom. 'Can anyone tell me how this thing goes?' he asked. One or two had a fair idea and were invited to explain to the others. Discussion. Questions. A bond formed. From then on the ground was clear to make the motor-cycle a foundation for a course of general education. How many miles to the gallon? (Arithmetic) What is the right pressure for tyres? What is air pressure? (Physics) What is high-octane gasoline? (Chemistry) How would you travel round the world by motor-cycle and ship? (Geography) Who invented the motor-cycle and when? (History) What does it feel like to be riding fast and free (Poetry) Who can tell me something about X? (Communication) What is insurance? What must you do if you have an accident? (Civics) A library about cars and bikes in one corner of the hut (Literature) Posters and drawings (Art) A wall newspaper (Current Affairs) The whole a confluent curriculum organized around shared interest. Gradually the adolescents' attitude of 'Let's spoil everything' changed into attention and purpose. The young men began to take an interest in learning about life and the world. One day, Sid, the erstwhile leader of the spoilers, came up to the teacher in the playground and said: 'If any of them try to take the Mickey, just let me know, sir.'

The real challenge came unexpectedly when the teacher had a puncture on his way to school and arrived half-an-hour late. Fearful that his exuberant mob would have torn the place apart without his steadying presence, he parked his motor-cycle and approached the hut. Not a sound. The worst had surely happened. The Head must have heard the din and taken them all into the school rumble room – used as a temporary store for impossible pupils. The teacher opened the door. There they all were, good as gold, with his 'protector' sitting at the teacher's desk and the others quietly busy with something or other. Sid stood up promptly. 'Been getting on, sir,' he said. 'Thought you might be having a bit of trouble with the bike.' The barbarians had become civilized. They had learnt how to learn and might, with luck, consider themselves capable of going on learning.

The second story is much shorter. One of the science specialists was down to teach 'General Science' to the non-academics. After yet another fruitless session, he was heard to say: 'You can't teach that lot any science. All they are interested in is motor-cycles.' The two cases mark the difference between pupil-based education and curriculum-based schooling.

Another example of a missed opportunity comes from a student-teacher. He had been sitting in on a science lesson. Some of the pupils were attending, several were not, and some were showing their lack of interest to the point of rudeness. The student-teacher noticed that, throughout the lesson, a boy in the corner was avidly reading a book, oblivious to the considerable hubbub that was going on. When the lesson was over, he approached the boy to find he was absorbed in a book on angling. Discussing the lesson with the teacher, he mentioned, 'That boy in the corner.' 'Oh, don't take any notice of him,' said the teacher. 'I've written him off long ago.' And yet angling is a world-wide sport and fish a major item of human diet.

Why are such opportunities frequently missed? The logic of motivation is that the secondary school curriculum should be there to serve the future orientation and present interests of the pupils. This is a complete reversal of the system in which the curriculum has been mapped out and the students are expected to fit into it. Ideally, the first two years at secondary school should be years of basic skills taught in the contexts of real-life situations, supplemented by a lively exploration of personal potentialities and environmental possibilities. To enhance stimulation, there should be plenty of new and unexpected experiences. As Dr Mia Kellmer Pringle has pointed out in *The Needs of Children*, the need for new experiences is a *basic* developmental need. By the end of the first two years, the pupils should have a good general grasp of what the world is like and be beginning to form ideas of what they want to do in it. They are then ready to take off in terms of their desired future. Sometimes, of course, this exploratory period will be covered in a Middle School.

The application of developmental and motivational principles to the upper forms of secondary schools requires that personal aspirations and interests should be the foundation of the curriculum, with subject and study groups made up on the basis of ability and shared purpose rather than age. It means the teachers knowing very much more about every individual than they commonly do at present. (That is an educational necessity anyway if we are to keep the adolescents with us.) It means more pastoral concern on the part of all teachers, and enough teachers to make this possible. That should be no obstacle if the country is really serious about giving all its adolescents a proper chance of growing and developing. The alternative will be an expanding expenditure of money, man-power and resources trying to contain the increasing number of disaffected, demotivated adolescents who, if we fail to take account of *their* aims, will do their best to wreck *ours*.

Thus the best hope for effective secondary education for all is personalized, confluent education. Such a re-programming will not banish the comfortably familiar subject areas from the timetable; nor will it reduce subject standards; it *will* ensure that those taking whatever curriculum they follow are committed learners. That would give a new vitality to the whole system. And it will make possible very much better relationships between teachers and students.

The realization that secondary education needs radical transformation is today world-wide. For example, an educational organization centred in Japan gives these new directions for education as its basic aims:

From education for knowledge to education for wisdom.

From one-sided education to education for the whole person.

86

From education of limited duration to lifelong integrated education.

From study of traditional culture to education for the creation of culture.

These aims are offered as an alternative to the hard-driving, academic system which eats into the life of youth while falling short in concern for the attainment of competent, relaxed maturity, and often generates a distaste for learning.

'If only they *wanted* to learn' is the desperate cry of so many young teachers. The tragedy is that they *do* want to learn, but that too few schools give sufficient attention to tapping the potential for growth of those who do not fit tidily into the traditional structures of schooling. It is not a matter of dropping all structure – that produces chaos – but of getting the structure carefully shaped to serve young people's needs within the actual perspectives of the contemporary world.

9

THE EDUCATIVE COMMUNITY

For every adolescent, secondary education should be an exciting and fulfilling staging post on the road to maturity. Behind lies childhood; ahead, the adult world with all its enchanting possibilities for being, doing, exploring, and relating. The family background – which is immensely important in the growth process – varies from the excellent to the disastrous. This gives children an uneven start, but, through our schools, we can make sure that all our young adults have the experience of belonging to a friendly, purposeful, civilized community while they are finding their feet in life, getting a valid perspective on the wider world, learning to associate happily with others, developing capabilities, finding ways of contributing, acquiring a set of values, discovering personal identity, and growing up generally. Through such experiences the essential, noncognitive skills of life are learnt, which are the major factors in personal competence. In his book, *Inequality*, Christopher Jencks, following an elaborate American research into what leads to success in life, wrote: 'The evidence reviewed suggests that noncognitive attributes may play a larger role than cognitive skills in determining economic success or failure. The evidence of our senses tells us that noncognitive traits also contribute far more than cognitive skills to the quality of human life and the extent of human happiness. We therefore believe that the noncognitive effects of schooling are likely to be more important than the cognitive effects.' Jencks points out that the research gives no clues to the source and detailed consequences of acquiring noncognitive skills, but there can be little doubt that noncognitive skills are developed in real situations involving people and problems, and manifest their effectiveness in later life by appropriate responses in similar situations.

Schools get into difficulties – and fail their pupils – when they allow their academic aims to take precedence over their developmental and social purposes. All should have careful attention. A secondary school's justification for existence is to serve as an evocative milieu for total adolescent growth. It should not be judged, or judge itself, mainly by scholastic successes. Results may look nice in the local papers, but only serve to give more to those who have, while taking away from those who have not. The school should also be judged by the quality of its community life, including what happens to those members of the school who are most in need of help and encouragement. The really searching question about a secondary school is not 'How many A levels, O levels and CSE's did your pupils score at the examination?' but 'What have you been doing, during the past year, for your inadequate, ineffective and isolated pupils?' These are not, of course, alternative questions. A truly educative school community will carry along its scholastic and social programmes with equal vigour, often unifying them through the way it conducts its affairs.

A good example of this is shown in those schools which deal with their remedial problems in the basic skills by asking for volunteers from the upper forms to help the stumbling and the stuck on an each-one-teach-one basis. This is of great benefit to both senior and junior partners. The children who have fallen behind respond well and the senior pupils learn the valuable lesson of caring for those less able than themselves. This is just one example of community help. Caring for one another is the root principle of the educative school community. We cannot expect children to care about their school if they do not feel cared for within the school. Nor can we help adolescents to become fully human personalities if the community in which they are educated is not built on the human values of caring and concern. All the staff, not only school counsellors, and all the pupils, are involved in developing these values within the school.

A deeply damaging hypocrisy of the school that treats academic attainment as its primary value is that, however much it may talk of *esprit de corps* on the playing field, or in out-of-school activities, the principle for the classroom is *esprit de moi* – the egocentric, competitive drive. In schools, as in industry, it is an illusion that competition is what achieves results. Competition is always divisive in its ultimate consequences. Competition is a stimulus but it is cooperation that gets things done. The community role of an individual is to contribute what he, or she, has to give in the setting of cooperative purpose. A modern education should be concerned with developing together individual achievement and social contribution.

Accordingly, along with friendliness and caring in the educative school community come cooperation and contribution. 'I like everyone to have a job,' a headmaster told me, 'then no child can be absent without feeling missed.' This, in its turn, depends on the social structure of the school. The natural social habitat for a human being is a small group in which everyone feels known and valued. For many children, one of the great shocks of starting secondary education is that they leave behind in the primary school a stable 'family' group and suddenly find themselves in an impersonal establishment which shuttles them from place to place, from teacher to teacher, without providing them with any friendly human base. This is a disastrous set-back for the development of many children. It is not easy to be sure that every pupil has a secure social base in a large school. Year groups are too large. House groupings may be little more than a way of generating rather phoney competitive loyalties, unrelated to human relationships and individual needs. The best arrangement is probably permanent tutor groups of mixed ages, in which the seniors are encouraged to act as older friends to the young ones. Such groups provide continuity and security – as long as the group is kept small enough to give a sense of belonging, and as long as its members spend enough time together to develop a sense of social solidarity. This involves roles for the groups in addition to keeping registers, collecting money and such utilitarian tasks.

One possibility is tutor group homework sessions, in which helping one another is a recognized procedure. This is not only a good social arrangement in itself but also is educationally preferable to homework dashed off on the top of the bus, done in a cold bedroom or crowded sitting-room, or by ringing up friends to find out the answers to sums and the translations of language passages – all regular features of the current scene. Other solutions can be found by way of providing for every pupil a friendly, supportive, enduring and purposeful *small* group as the social unit of school life. What is monstrous is that some secondary schools are so unaware of the social and developmental needs of young people that no such groups exist – school life is passed in conditions of social chaos. Instead of organizing the school in groups of mixed ages, a teacher may stay with her group as they move up through the school. This is an excellent arrangement so long as enough time is provided for the group to get together. One finds instances of such grouping when meetings occur only once a week for ten or fifteen minutes!

An excuse often advanced to explain gaps in social provision is: 'We haven't time.' Why all the rush? In our frantic, over-active, butterfly-minded civilization, schools should aim to be friendly, relaxed places where there is time to do everything that is necessary to help young people to become self-confident, self-contained human beings. Rush = Inefficiency say the exponents of sound industrial management. This is true of schools too. Rush means either that too many things are being attempted at once – with the resulting skimping of essentials – or that the structure of the establishment is not closely enough matched to its proper educational purposes. So we come back to the selection of priorities. Whatever goes, the humanity must remain. If schooling is not, throughout, a humanizing process, it is failing in its essential role.

A school community built on friendliness, cooperation and contribution is, *pari passu*, a democratic establishment – in which all members share some of the responsibility for what is going on – rather than an autocratic one, in which the subordinate members are left with no choice but to conform or rebel. School democracy is sometimes thought to be just a matter of setting up pupils' councils which meet from time to time with a formal agenda. Such councils can be useful in generating significant feed-back, or they may be empty rituals which do little but confirm the futility of the 'representational illusion'. Democracy in school at once comes to life when the pupils are brought in on the day-to-day problems that the school community throws up.

One school, for example, found itself with an acute litter problem after opening its own tuck-shop. The caretaker complained that he was not going to stand for the extra work created. We will not here go into the morality of tuck-shops as tooth-rotting institutions, but instead consider what the school did about the litter. A headmaster's harangue at assembly, supported by notices to the tutor groups, produced a very temporary improvement. Next followed a stiff warning 'If the untidiness goes on, the tuck-shop will be closed.' There was no improvement and closure followed. The tuckshop was re-opened after a week and the nuisance returned almost at once.

At that point, the Head asked the senior students to investigate the problem. They approached a member of staff to act as sponsor for a Working Party which was composed of four senior students and a representative from each year. The Working Party heard evidence from the caretaker, the people running the tuck-shop, members of staff who patrolled the playing area, and pupils. The central question that needed answering was why the pupils would not put their sweet packings in the wire cages provided in the playgrounds. What emerged from the Working Party was that the cages were wrongly positioned. When the bell went, the patrons of the tuck-shop were disinclined to hunt for a rubbish cage but dropped the wrappings either where they were or on their way to the classrooms. The suggestion was made that the cages should be re-located on either side of the entrances to the school and that senior students should supervise their use at the end of free times. That cured the problem.

The way this litter crisis was dealt with is a good example of a school taking responsibility for itself. Harangues and the punitive approach failed because they did not get to the source of the apparent carelessness. The Working Party was successful on two counts: it gave students a useful experience of this mode of democratic procedure, and it found the social solution to a social problem. With the vote now at eighteen, where are our young adults supposed to learn about both representative and participant democracy if not in helping to run, and improve, the school community? How many schools are adequate on this score?

The experience of self-regulation is educationally of great value for young people. Discipline in a community is best maintained not by isolated rules and punishments but by the acceptance of responsibility for one's own and one another's behaviour. The role of the adults in a school community is not to be the punishers but to generate feelings of social responsibility by mobilizing the community's own wisdom. Most people – including adolescents – will behave reasonably if the circumstances are reasonable. In contrast, when there is a staff-versus-pupil atmosphere in a school, there is no incentive for the pupils to guide their own or others' behaviour; the operative principle is simply not to be found out. A self-regulating community has a built-in bias towards common concern and common sense. As we saw in Chapter Two, adolescents are perfectly capable of controlling their own communities in the general interest when a situation exists which encourages the acceptance of responsibility. On the other hand, adolescents who are treated like children will behave like children. It is within the framework of a democratic school community that opportunities readily arise for those relationships and encounters which promote the development of personal competence.

Something we must respect if we wish for the cooperation of adolescents is their dignity. This is why corporal punishment defeats its own ends. The young will not tolerate a disregard for their personal dignity. There can be no real respect for individual dignity in a situation when the members of one group in a community have the unilateral right to beat the members of another group. This has been recognized long ago in all institutions except educational institutions, and, in most countries, the schools too have come into line with modern attitudes. Not, alas, in Britain. When I was a young teacher, I once saw a headmaster beat a boy. It was repulsively undignified for both beater and beaten, and certainly in breach of Article 5 of the Universal Declaration of Human Rights. Schools that still use cane or tawse cannot be expected to give it up on demand. They could be given a reasonable time – say two years – in which to replace force and fear by civilized social management.

Some schools are admirable examples of such management. The Deputy Head of a co-educational comprehensive school was going up the stairs to a class she was about to teach when she met a young lady in an obvious fury coming down. The teacher asked what was the matter: 'He insulted me in front of the class,' the girl said angrily. 'I'm going straight to the headmaster.' And she did. She complained that the teacher, a young man, had made a caustic remark about the clothes he had seen her wearing in the town the night before. The Head saw the girl and the young teacher together and sorted the matter out. The idea of pupils being allowed to complain about the behaviour of the staff makes some teachers cringe. Why exactly, though, should parents and teachers be allowed to complain *ad lib* about adolescents while the adolescents are expected to sit on their feelings? Openness is never a threat to discipline; rather the reverse, provided that the civilities of human exchange are maintained *on both sides*. The school where the incident described above occurred is a happy school with a high standard of discipline, but where everybody has a right to justice and, therefore, a right to be heard. The young teacher needed to learn that he must respect the feelings of those in his charge. Failing that, he could have become a source of constant resentment. Disrespect on the side of the teacher and imposed respect on the side of the pupil is not a personal but a power relationship. The creative interaction is human reciprocity. According to reports from students on teaching practice, who are often shocked by what they see going on, this elementary principle of inter-personal relationships is still not properly understood in many secondary schools.

Of course, at the heart of the community life of the school, and extending out into fruitful contacts beyond the school, is the quality of the face-to-face relationships between student and teacher. Right from birth the interaction between child and adult is educationally of great significance. At the adolescent stage, an important component of it is a sense of shared purpose in achieving the skills and development which the adolescent wants to acquire. The sort of characteristics that help the formation of a fruitful pupil-teacher bond has been investigated on several occasions. The gist of American inquiries gives this sort of profile of the teacher adolescents hope for:

Likes teenagers
Has enthusiasm and drive
Is generous in approval
Gets along well with people
Is friendly and tolerant
Is fair and impartial
Has a good sense of humour
Is patient and even-tempered
Treats pupils as individuals
Teaches well

This list can be summed up as follows: Adolescents appreciate teachers who are easy to like, who respect them as individuals, and who mean business as teachers. Given those three it is likely that the creative bond will be formed. Teachers benefit from this every bit as much as the students.

A humane, democratic school is a truly open society. It shares information freely, maintains good communications, and is careful to promote the feedback without which no community can stay healthy. Feed-back means that machinery exists to bring resentments, irritations and complaints into the open where they can be faced as social problems. The resentments of individual pupils are, of course, to be

95

included. Where a difficult individual pupil is concerned, the Head, tutor or counsellor may have to draw out the feedback from that particular student by a careful search for what lies behind the bad behaviour. An Irish headmistress, now retired, who ran her school with a genial robust frankness explained to me how she always asked the nuisances what she could do for them, rather along these lines: 'You aren't behaving very well, are you? So we must be failing you in some way. I want you to tell me what we can do to help you stop making such a nuisance of yourself.' She would then coax the boy or girl into a discussion and often discovered a deep sense of resentment or injustice that was long overdue for an airing. In any human community, to get the resentments out in the open – staff resentments as well as pupil resentments – goes a long way towards improving relationships and raising morale. There are always resentments around somewhere. Either they are uncovered and dispersed or they fester and fatten behind the scenes. A recent inquiry conducted among the secondary schools of Lincolnshire revealed that wide discrepancies may exist between what Principals think is going on in their schools and how the pupils evaluate what is happening. Organized feed-back can close such gaps in understanding.

But getting itself into good human order is only the beginning for a school. It has to aim to be a community within the wider community with which it has formed all kinds of relationships: offering opportunities, providing facilities, sharing activities. This concept of the community school is proving itself in a score of different ways. It helps to heal the social fragmentation which has been increasingly destructive during this century. It saves a school from the isolated monasticism which is still found, but which is not an appropriate educational milieu for young people growing up in the modern world. It creates a bridge between the world of adolescents and the world of adults which can only lead to greater understanding and tolerance on both sides. It opens up opportunities for the students to make more contact with the wider community in their education. And it creates for the students a broad community base through which they may relate themselves to the life of the nation and the world.

Raven's research shows that young people are themselves eager to extend the school's contacts with the community. He gave the boys and girls of his sample a questionnaire containing 50 items and asked them which items they thought 'the school should do more of.' Returns revealed the young people's eagerness to get beyond the confines of the classroom and school. The top ten items from the boys' results were as follows.

THE SCHOOL SHOULD DO MORE OF:	PERCENTAGE SELECTING ITEM
1. Encourage friendships between boys and girls, for example by running co-educational hobbies and social clubs.	80
2. Take you on visits to factories or offices or other places to see the different sorts of jobs there are and what work is like.	80
3. Educational visits in connection with your subjects – such as to see chemical plants, museums and theatres.	76
4. Introduce you to new subjects e.g. philosophy, sociology, archaeology.	73
5. Advise parents to give sex education to their children.	71
6. Have outside speakers about careers and other educational topics.	69
7. Run courses for adults as well as young people.	67

8. Teach you about bringing up
children, home repairs,   66
decorating and so on.

9. Teach you about a wide range
of cultures and philosophies so
that your own can be seen to be   65
only one of many.

10. Help you to understand the
implications and responsibilities   64
of marriage.

The percentages for girls varied from the boys, but not by
much. The girls' top ten included nine of the boys' items.
The additional item in the girls' list is: Take you on holidays
in this country and abroad: 65%. This replaces the boys'
item of 'Advise parents to give sex education to their children' which, in the girls' list, comes 13th with 59%. The
preferences show clearly the adolescents' love of mobility,
mentioned in chapter two, and also the future orientation of
their thinking. Adolescents are more than ready to use the
school as a base for educating themselves by relating to the
wider community.

The experience of living in a happy, purposeful school
community is not only pleasant in itself; it is also an
important part of social education. To secure such experience for young people is to armour them against the isolation
and fragmentation of modern society at the same time as
equipping them to promote good community life wherever
they may find themselves. A capacity for responsibility grows
through participation.

How does a good school community come into existence?
The answer seems to be that it grows from the personality,
integrity, humanity and creative purpose of the head teacher.
A group of Her Majesty's Inspectors carried out a survey of
ten schools of different types but all with outstanding repu-
tations. The final section of their pamphlet, *Ten Good
Schools* published in 1977, serves to show the crucial role of
the Principal in creating a humane, purposeful school. In the

section entitled 'Climate and Leadership' it says: 'The schools visited differ in very many respects as institutions, although each can demonstrate its quality in its aims, in oversight of pupils, in curriculum design, in standards of teaching and academic achievements and in its links with the local community. What they all have in common is effective leadership and a 'climate' that is conducive to growth. The schools see themselves as places designed for learning; they take trouble to make their philosophies explicit for themselves and to explain them to parents and pupils; the foundation of their work and corporate life is an acceptance of shared values.

'Emphasis is laid on consultation, team work and participation, but, without exception, the most important single factor in the success of these schools is the quality of leadership of the head. Without exception, the heads have qualities of imagination and vision, tempered by realism, which have enabled them to sum up not only their present situation but also attainable future goals. They appreciate the need for specific educational aims, both social and intellectual, and have the capacity to communicate these to staff, pupils and parents, to win their assent and to put their own policies into practice. Their sympathetic understanding of staff and pupils, their accessibility, good humour and sense of proportion and their dedication to their task has won them the respect of parents, teachers and taught. They are conscious of the corruption of power and though ready to take final responsibility they have made power-sharing the keynote of their organisation and administration. Such leadership is crucial for success and these schools are what their heads and staffs have made them.'

The reference to 'the corruption of power' is to be noted. Few positions remaining in society still carry such autocratic authority as is vested in a head teacher.

It seems, then, that the quality of school community depends largely upon the quality of the Principal as a human being and his, or her, capacity to stimulate and unify the energies and abilities of his staff. One would expect, therefore, that the greatest care would go into the selection of Principals. In some countries it does. In Britain, however, we cling to an antiquated system which no self-respecting business organization would use for selection of key personnel. From the applications received, 'The Office' makes a short list of half-a-dozen or so. These candidates are then put up in turn before a selection committee for interview. This is a notoriously chancy system. Fortunately many good Principals survive this process but it also gives the clever window-dresser, and the man with little to offer but a fistful of high academic qualifications, a good chance of getting accepted. It is ludicrous that a group of earnest and sincere people should be expected to select, in thirty minutes, the right individual from the short list – someone who is destined to affect the lives of thousands of children throughout their school years. The supreme quality in a Principal – the *sine qua non* – is the ability to build a school into a harmonious educative community, yet it is precisely this quality that cannot be effectively tested by the method used. The result is that individuals who are too autocratic, bad with relationships, or lacking in imagination may succeed in becoming Principals while individuals who are well endowed with the essential human qualities are passed over. The only sure way to select Principals is to observe them in action with other people, either in the school situation itself, or in arranged circumstances, such as a selection week-end. The secondary system of this country will remain seriously short of educative communities until better head teacher selection systems are devised and used.

That we have a number of first-class Principals who manage to control an excessively examination-orientated secondary system in the interests of both staff and pupils is more the result of luck than the selection system. As for the inadequate ones, and the plain bad ones who get through this tatty net, these do calamitous damage in total security, until retirement rescues them from the ill-fitting robes of high responsibility. It would be better, surely, if these were given a golden handshake and encouraged to retire early.

This chapter has made little mention of subjects, curricula, examinations and other traditional absorptions of secondary education. It has been about something more fundamental than the components of schooling; its concern has been the vitally important social climate of adolescent growth. Subjects and tests have their place in the overall educational scheme but the proper outcome of secondary education is not overtaxed heads but young people well equipped for life. Such a desirable result depends on the careful establishment of a good community life and its constant presence behind the nuts and bolts of the learning process. Moreover, learning takes place with greater facility in a happy, relaxed atmosphere where people are in good relationships with one another. Thus, efficient education and good community life go together.

At the time of going to press, the vital importance of those subtle factors summed up by the phrase 'the ethos of the school' has been given new edge by the work of Professor Michael Rutter and his colleagues, reported in *Fiften Thousand Hours*. There can no longer be any doubt that the attainments and behaviour of adolescents – their humanization and maturation – can be profoundly influenced by the social organization, friendliness, sense of purpose, shared responsibility, and interpersonal relationships offered by the schools they attend, irrespective of familial and neighbourhood influences and the sort of buildings housing the schools. Education in the future – indeed society itself – will stand or fall by our success, or failure, to raise the quality of experience within our secondary schools.

That being so, how are we to accommodate, without undue stress, the bogey of the educational process – assessment? We will now take a look at how we can humanize this.

10

HUMANIZING ASSESSMENT

It would be hard to think of a more devastating way of destroying the joy of learning among the young than the threat of low grading in comparisons with their fellows. It is a mortal stab at self-esteem, which kills personal confidence and parental expectations at one thrust. Because of it, a not inconsiderable number of breakdowns and suicides occur among the young every year. Assessing individual attainment is something that should be carried out with great delicacy and sensitivity. It can only be justified within the process of education if it does not damage young people, and if it is accurate and fair. The means commonly in use in Great Britain today, though not only in Britain, meet none of these criteria. As a system of personal assessment, it is basically unsound.

Its most perfidious dishonesty is that it seems to claim – never overtly, but by implication – not only to prove attainment in specific knowledge and skills but to brand students as being on different levels of quality and potential as human beings. This, at any rate, is how the system operates and few in authority go out of their way to refute it. Even worse, the fateful judgement – double first, A level grade C, failed CSE, or whatever – is stamped home for good at a particular time as if implying that a human being is an immutable entity. It takes into no account the fact that people change as time passes and unsuspected elements previously hidden find a way to grow. Michael Frayn, the author and dramatist, writes of a teacher he was fortunate enough to meet at a time when he was going through a bad patch at school: 'Mr

Brady first taught me when I was bottom in everything. By giving exaggerated encouragement with ridiculously high marks for essays, he reconnected me to the world. He was no academic but showed great imagination in getting through to a difficult child. It was to him that I dedicated my first book.'

Knowing what we do today, we can recognize in this a right-hemisphere dominant responding to the creativity of a pupil. But suppose Michael Frayn had not received the encouragement he needed, would he have taken off again and grown into the creative and versatile person he became? And what might have happened to Jimmy Boyle (page 76) if he had met, at about the same age, a teacher who had discovered and encouraged his creative flair? Who can say? Of this we can be sure, this irrevocable grading of individuals puts a permanent blight on the lives of those assessed as inferior. The damaging prophecies become self-fulfilling.

The great fraud of it is that the semblance of objectivity is studiously maintained inspite of the fact that its 'accuracy' in assessment is highly dubitable. A Yorkshire headmaster, as reported by John Hipkin in *Verdict on the Facts*, entered twenty-eight of his English candidates for the ordinary level, General Certificate of Education examinations set by two different Examining Boards. 'One Board failed 25 and passed 3 of his pupils; the other failed 1 and passed 27.' The situation is just as vague in the hallowed field of the first class honours degree. Consider, for example these comparisons.

DATE	PROPORTION OF 1ST CLASS HONOURS AWARDED	
1962 (all universities)	To mathematics students	14%
	To social studies students	3%
1968 (contrast of two universities)	at Kent University	17%
	at Keele University	4.9%

If there is anything in the entire educational system that is treated as special proof of higher human quality it is, surely, the first class honours degree, yet it is as vulnerable to varying conditions as any other academic qualification. The pretence of accuracy makes things all the worse. The hierarchy of success runs like this:

CLASS

I
II (i)
II (ii)
III
Pass
Fail

This gives an appearance of mathematical precision which is unjustified. The truth seems to be that by choosing his subject and university carefully a student can more than treble his chances of getting a first. Grades in lower examinations are equally imprecise. A cold in the head, or a lucky question, can make all the difference quite apart from the impossibility of completely eliminating the idiosyncratic variations in judgement of those who mark the papers.

Even so, it is argued, examinations successfully passed prove that candidates have made an important store of knowledge their own. But is that really so? Roy Cox of the London University Institute of Education reported in a lecture: 'Professor Drever, who was at Edinburgh University, did an experiment with Psychology and Physics students in which an identical multi-choice exam was given again, without warning, after a six weeks interval. Of the 300 students taking part, the average drop in marks was catastrophic. 120 who passed the first time failed the second.'

We can assume, therefore, that it is yet one more educational illusion that we can accurately and fairly grade *people* by the traditional type of examination. What about the non-traditional innovations? These take many forms. One variation from the essay test is to examine in whole, or in part, by multiple-choice questions. Here, for example, is one such question set in a University of London G.C.E. O level History paper in 1978:

104

When Mussolini organized unions and employers into corporations his main aim was to:
A give workers the right to strike
B increase the influence of the communists
C satisfy the opposition parties in parliament
D strengthen the state's control of the economy
E weaken the power of the fascists

The candidate has to indicate which answer he thinks is correct by pencilling in a space on a score sheet.

Multiple-choice questions are very tempting for examiners. They permit a wide range of the field of study to be covered in a short time. They test the candidate's level of information and, to some extent, his judgement. As everyone does all the questions differences arising from a choice of questions are eliminated. And they are easy to mark – an alluring feature when the number of candidates is large and computers are at hand to do a quick job on the scoring. Their weakness, and it is a serious one, is that the whole examination process is mechanical. No creativity is required; you either know it or you don't. To give imagination and creativity a chance, a multiple-choice paper needs balancing with essay-type answers, or with problems for which there is no cut-and-dried solution. And that takes us back to the point from which we started.

Another alternative to the frantic scribblings of timed examinations is continuous assessment. In this, some or all of the candidate's regular work goes towards his final grading. That seems fair and sensible, and it eliminates the advantages gained by those who are good at last minute swotting. On the other hand, continuous assessment can play havoc with student-teacher relationships as the teacher's grading of any piece of work raises or lowers the candidate's expectations for a good result. This can undermine relaxed study, and experimental approaches. Instead of being freer because the final examination is no longer there, the candidate may feel he must strive for approved conformity all the time.

Projects to be carried out at the students' own pace are

another possibility. This gives time to produce something of real quality in place of the hastily thrown together examination room answer. The difficulty here is that it is not easy to assess how much of the final product is the students' own work. Forewarning the candidates of the field to be examined is yet another way of encouraging close study. But, in that case, why coop up the candidates at all for what is virtually a replay of something they have already done in their own time? We are back to swotting and regurgitation in a less anxiety-ridden form. The awful fear of not being able to do any of the questions may have been removed but, nevertheless, it still adds up to a memory test.

The 'open book' examination has also been suggested. Real life, it is argued, is about using sources of information intelligently, so why not examine for that quality rather than for the ability to memorize material. This would certainly save English Literature candidates from endlessly going over the same texts until they become a bore instead of a pleasure. This, presumably, was in Alan Ayckbourn's mind when he said he hoped 'Not to have my plays included as part of the school syllabus and know what it's like to be loathed by a whole generation of school children.' A version of the open book approach to History is to present the candidates with a set of original documents and ask them questions which require an intelligent interpretation of the extracts. There seems a lot to be said for open book examinations but they do not seem to be popular with either examiners or teachers. Exactly why is not very clear. Some teachers say it makes the examination too easy for the able candidates, but harder for the weaker ones, who can no longer be crammed for likely questions. It certainly means that setting papers calls for more imagination. There do not, however, seem to be any sound educational arguments against open book examinations. They need more intelligent comprehension than those requiring mainly memorization, and that change is highly desirable educationally.

These are only some of the experiments in examining which we have seen over the past couple of decades. Yet none of these, either alone or in combination with others, carries the conviction that *this* is the perfect answer.

When reforms fail to produce satisfactory solutions we can usually assume that the proposed changes are not fundamental enough. What then is fundamental in the testing-examining-assessing-selecting aspect of an educational system? Can we arrive at a method which is consistent with the sort of principles of growth, development, and good teacher-pupil relationships with which this book has been concerned? I think we can. For a start, we have to make a clear distinction between competence as a person and knowledge of a particular subject area, or skill in a certain function. What society needs, in any career capacity, is the assurance of personal competence plus evidence of special knowledge and skill. Society needs to know that, say, a surgeon has at his disposal all the skills that a surgeon needs. It is also desirable that the surgeon should have attained a high standard of competence as a human being, otherwise a good deal of his special knowledge and skill may be marred. But these two elements of 'a good surgeon' are distinct and should be treated as such. Knowledge and skill examinations, related to specific functions, are unavoidable in a technically advanced society, but they should never be regarded as tests of people. This is a first principle for all revised examination procedures.

What particular areas of knowledge and skill a student embarks upon should arise naturally from his present interests. It should have nothing to do with putting together a parcel of passes so that he can trade himself off as this, or that, quality of human being; it should be a personal choice related to his own growth, and his own aspirations for the future. If the secondary school offered, right from the start, plenty of opportunities for exploration and achievement at different levels of complexity, a mixed diet educationally would be a good prospect without compulsion. And if the schools would set out to keep natural curiosity alive as a major purpose, as indeed it should be, one could expect, for each individual, a broad experiential, life-related, self-chosen curriculum from which some special skills would grow as the students' abilities, interests and aspirations unfolded.

107

'That,' someone may object, 'is what we have now.' It is not. What we have now is a system of graded examinations into which a maximum number of candidates are squeezed, with the growth of the individual child as a person receiving minimal consideration. What is proposed instead is a system in which the growth and purposes of students are central, with the option open for the students to test themselves out with any sort of examination, if they want to do so. He, or she, uses the examination; not the other way round.

In such a system, the student would be measured, and would measure himself, against his own previous achievement and not by comparison with other individuals. It is said that students like to know where they come. This is true of those within sight of the top places; it is not true of the rest. Does any student really care whether he is twenty-second or twenty-third in a group of twenty-five? Yet he does care when the teacher shows him the way to improvement in a field in which he wants to be good. Competition for class places is a corruption of the growth process. The school that depends on inter-personal competition and the incentive of examinations to keep children up to scratch has simply failed to tap the personal aspirations of its students. It is vitally important that the necessary motivational change should be made in our schools *now* because we are moving into a future when people who are not self-motivating will have a very poor chance of personal fulfilment.

This leads on to the system of assessment which is just coming onto the scene. We might call this co-operative assessment. This proposes that the teachers and students team up to help the students to achieve the aims which they aspire to and which it has been agreed are possible. The students then co-operate with the teachers in assessing and recording their own work and progress.

Jonathan Croall, Features Editor of the *Times Educational Supplement*, writing in *Where* for June 1978 on 'Why Exams?' sums up the situation: 'In the long term, perhaps the only genuinely fair method of assessment is one which avoids grading students against each other, and concentrates instead on each individual's weaknesses and strengths, on their social and personal qualities as well as their learning skills and achievement. In any such profile, a major element ought to be the student's own perception of what he or she has gained or lost through being at school. There ought also to be room for parents to add their thoughts on the same topic.'

We may notice that this sort of assessment is in complete accord with the purpose of improving relations 'on the job' between students and their teachers. The us-and-them goes out of the situation to be replaced by a sense of joint enterprise, with an increasing challenge to the student to take responsibility for his own progress. Dr W. D. Wall writes: 'These objectives (stimulation and evaluation) can be compassed by a system whereby effort and attainment are separately assessed and compared, not as between pupils, but by comparison with each pupil's own previous levels. Clearly this involves a more detailed knowledge of each pupil and a greater insight into the efforts he makes than are required by an arbitrary competitive system of marking. It involves, for example, the attempt by the teacher from time to time to review with each child the good qualities and the weak spots in his current work in a particular subject, and the attempt to bring him to see where improvements can be made and where greater effort is required. In turn this involves, as an essential part of the process of transferring to the pupil himself the means of judgement, the clear specification of objectives and criteria. These specifications can be in terms of particular masteries with appropriate tests or, of course, they can be goals laid down by the pupil himself for a piece of work on which he is engaged.'

The principle of pupil participation in assessment is a safeguard against teacher-based pupil grading becoming a source of estrangement and bitterness between teachers and students. In the summer of 1978 I found myself in the role of convener to a Youth Forum in America. All but one of the able high-school students who were members loathed the grading system. They saw it as unfair, a weapon teachers could use against students, and as a constant threat to the students' peace of mind. They also hated the multiple-choice tests and regarded the American College Test as a hit-or-miss affair which did not give them a chance to show their abilities. The one exception in the group did not agree with any of this. The difference turned out to be that, in his school, teachers and students were in continuous dialogue about assessment. The students felt they knew where they were and what they had to do, and that the teachers were there to help them. In this student's case, there was no sense of being at the mercy of the teachers which the other young members of the Forum had expressed so strongly. He felt himself to be in control of his destiny.

All this seems to lead towards student profiles as the most humane and least deleterious way of evaluating personality and attainments for university and job selection. Profiles do not necessarily exclude subject examinations or objective tests but shift them into a different perspective. Various kinds of profiles have been suggested, or are actually in use. The essentials seem to be:

1. A report on general personality and competence.
2. A record of specific personal achievements, and responsibilities undertaken.
3. A record of any skills or subjects that have been successfully developed to examination standard.

The report on (1) should not, of course, be from a single teacher, but should be an assessment that has been agreed by those who have been most closely involved with the student. The purpose of the profile is to be as positive as possible – concerned with revealing competencies rather than with exposing weaknesses.

It all takes time, of course, but, as has been noted earlier, if we do not provide sufficient staffing to permit caring, relaxed mutuality between teachers and pupils at the secondary school stage, then we shall fail to produce adults capable of finding fulfilment and happiness in the changed circumstances of the sort of future now imminent, and capable of guiding society along the paths of humanity, not to mention sustaining economic viability.

Fortunately there is a growing mood for change in methods of assessment, partly because the products of the traditional system do not always live up to expectations. Profile assessments have already been successfully tried out at university level, as under Professor Denys Hinton at the University of Aston, Birmingham. Another initiative is that of the Manpower Services in seeking ways to record the actual abilities of non-academic young people. Yet another is that initiated by Tyrrell Burgess at the School of Independent Study in the North East London Polytechnic, where some students, selected by informal means, attain standards in the Diploma of Higher Education just as good as those of students satisfying the usual examination requirements. Some local Education Authorities are experimenting with recording systems of assessment, while up-to-date proposals for pupils and teachers in secondary schools to develop individualized programmes and records are shortly to be published by Macmillan under the title: *The Outcome of Compulsory Education*, edited by Tyrrell Burgess and Elizabeth Adams. Leading industrialists, as we noted earlier (page 24) are interested in exploring the use of profiles for job selection. It is to be hoped that such activity marks the beginning of a new, juster era of measuring human quality and an end to the academic obstacle race.

For schools, the essential change is one of attitude. It is doubtful whether the humanization of education can co-exist with competitive examinations and tests but, so long as exams continue, they too should change – in the direction of encouraging fully aware individuals. Young people crammed with information about two or three subjects in isolation from the rest of human experience cannot be considered educated. The importance of teaching any subject, at any level, in the context of life has already been emphasized (Chapter 8). Examiners should catch up with this educational requirement in the way they frame their questions. At present some of them are edging forward in the right direction without seeming to follow any consistent educational principles.

Here, for example, is a traditional type of question from a London University GCE Physics paper for June, 1978. 'When a body is totally or partially immersed in a fluid it

111

experiences an upthrust equal to the weight of the fluid displaced.'
Describe an experiment which you could perform in a laboratory to verify the above statement for an object which sinks in water, showing clearly how your measurement would be used.'

Such a question merely invites repetition of what the teacher has demonstrated – or should have done. Here is another question from the same paper:
'Name the forces of energy involved, and state clearly the changes in them, in the following processes:
(i) An aircraft lands on the deck of an aircraft carrier and a hook catches on one of a series of wires stretching across the deck. The wire becomes greatly extended and the aircraft slows quickly in the short distance available.
(ii) A car runs off the road and collides with a large tree which brings it quickly to rest with damage to the front of the vehicle.
Explain in physical terms how in situation (ii) the wearing of seat-belts by driver and passenger might help to prevent serious injuries.'

This question is at least as searching academically as the first one quoted, but it puts the scientific principles involved in the context of real situations and tests not only memory but thinking. Do examiners include questions that are purely memory based in order to meet the needs of cramming teachers and crammed pupils? If so, it is an intention which encourages bad teaching.

A GCE History question from the Associated Examining Board, June 1978, takes the approach to the whole mind a stage further:
'Israel has offered to integrate the 300,000 Palestinian refugees in the Gaza region, and give them a choice between Israeli and Jordanian Nationality.'
Choose THREE of the following, and write for each a statement of reaction to this communiqué:
General Dyan, the Israeli Foreign Minister.
Colonel Gadafi of Libya.
President Sadat of Egypt.

King Hussein of Jordan.
A representative of the Palestinian guerillas.
A Palestinian refugee.
An Israeli living in Tel Aviv.'

Such a question is thoroughly contemporary, encourages socially-aware education, probes not only accurate knowledge but also imagination, intuition, and sensitivity. It tests the quality of the candidates' intellect as no mere reproduction exercise can do. A particularly interesting advance has been made in the alternative ordinary level paper 'Science and Socicty' set for the first time in June, 1978, by the Oxford and Cambridge Schools Examination Board. In Section A, this draws on both geographical and historical data, and, in Section B, gives a wide choice of questions on contemporary themes. One reads:

'Discuss man's use of the atmosphere (a) as a source of raw material, (b) as a source of energy and (c) as a sink for waste products.'

Another invites the candidates to write an essay on 'Science and religion'. The paper is confluent in approach, stimulates judgement and clarity of thought, calls upon the candidates to relate things together, spot significant patterns, and use value judgements and imagination. Furthermore, it is a paper that any well-read and broadly educated student could tackle. It is looking for alert intelligences, not crammed brains. Examinations, then, can encourage good education – rather than the reverse – so long as the questions offer educationally valid incentives to teachers and pupils. Both-subject teaching and examination questions need to become more confluent in approach.

It cannot be over-emphasized that the mode of assessment dictates the nature of the educational experience and the quality of the relationship between teacher and pupils. Assessment is not something separate – a tool – by which education may be evaluated; it acts upon the educational system so as to shape it in accordance with what the assessment demands. You cannot have, at one and the same time, education for personal growth and a totally impersonal system of assessment. Assessment should be a bond between

113

teachers and taught, not something which threatens and antagonizes.

To humanize assessment, then, we have to make of schooling a more co-operative enterprise between teachers and pupils, and an opportunity to develop the whole range of human competencies, leading up to informative profiles. This should be the pattern of things for the immediate future; it is the way to shed the dreary, and often unjust, grading techniques of traditional education.

11

THE BELIEF VACUUM

I have kept almost until last the most profound problem of education, and of our civilization – the collapse of traditional belief in western society and the failure to replace it with anything that is capable of lifting existence above the trivial. Talking of the workless adolescents in her area, a social worker recently said: 'They stand around unemployed and uninspired.' It is not the problem of unemployment – serious as it is – to which I want, at the moment, to draw attention but to everything implied by that word 'uninspired'. Human beings, especially the young, need a sense of inspiration. We yearn for the touch of wonder, of beauty, of greatness. We long to share in something that transcends ourselves, and we want to understand.

For the West, until very recently, these needs were met for most people by a religious world-view – the Judaeo-Christian ideology. Now this ideology has lost its grip on the human intellect. One reason for this is that the cosmology which sustained the old beliefs has been replaced by something entirely different. Belief and cosmology are, and always have been, inseparable. This is true of all nations and all ages: the sense of personal value, and the values by which people conduct their lives, have always had as their foundation a set of beliefs about the universe which 'explained everything'. The belief systems varied but their role in society was the same.

The quandary of the West is that the traditional religious belief system and our contemporary cosmological outlook have become incurably inconsistent with one another. And it has all happened quite fast. I was brought up in a country rectory, in the heart of rural East Anglia, over the fields from Eliot's 'Little Gidding'. All of us – farm workers, bosses, the local intelligentsia, not to mention the learned scholars who occasionally visited us from Cambridge – shared a belief in a simple cosmology, made up of Heaven, somewhere 'beyond the bright blue sky'; Earth, on which we had a temporary residence before going, at our deaths, to that very Heaven, if we were virtuous enough, or, if we were not, to Hell which was vaguely 'below'. We were not supposed to believe in this as a 'Just So' story, or as a symbolic presentation of the condition of man, but as the actual celestial geography of the universe as it affected the human individual. God was 'in heaven' and, all being well, we would 'go to heaven' when we died. The Lord's Prayer which we constantly repeated, the creed we said together, the hymns we sang all made this simple cosmology seem as certainly 'there' as the church in which we sang lustily – especially at Christmas, Easter and Harvest Festival.

Now the whole basis for those unsophisticated beliefs has gone – for good. Whatever efforts are made to transpose the Judaeo-Christian ideology to fit the contemporary world, its original cosmological foundation can never be restored. We now know that we live in a universe of inexpressible vastness, of which our sun is a medium-sized star swinging in space on the outer edges of a galaxy containing something in the order of 100,000,000,000 other stars; and the whole galaxy only one among thousands of millions of galaxies. We also have every reason to believe that, when conditions are right for life to emerge anywhere in this immense universe, it will do so, and that, where conditions are favourable, it will evolve to higher and higher forms of complexity and awareness, as on planet Earth.

Thus, although we are still short of the final confirmation by radio, or other, signals, which will take time – radio is not yet a hundred years old and the universe is *very* large – we can be virtually certain that intelligent life exists on some others of the billions of planets circling other stars. What then becomes of the idea of our 'own' God or of our 'own' redemption by the Son of God? Since life, wherever it emerges, will always be imperfect, because it is evolving, then every planet on which there is intelligent life will certainly be in need of great moral teachers. But can we conceive of a million planets saved from sin by a million crucifixions? No difficulty arises if we regard Jesus as a man who was a moral genius and a model of how to live; all kinds of problems appear if we try to combine our present knowledge of the universe with the idea of a unique Son of God saving the planet. In such ways as this the new cosmology is in conflict with traditional beliefs. This conflict is likely to intensify as time passes.

It is not only theologians who are faced with a problem of re-interpretation. Scientists, too, have lost the Newtonian certainties of the nineteenth century and find themselves struggling with an unexpectedly mobile and enigmatic universe. Today, whether people hold a religious or naturalistic view of existence, they have to adapt their thinking to a cosmological perspective which is fundamentally at odds with that held by the West in the past. Scientists find the adjustment easier than theologians because their business has always been search whereas, traditionally, theologians have been concerned with certainty. Some theologians seek to escape from the challenge to traditional belief by saying that it is still as true as ever it was if we regard it as symbolism rather than history. Mythological expression and symbolism are forms of truth when they carry a true message about human existence, but the symbolism should not conflict with established scientific knowledge or confusion must result. At present the Churches are maintaining both stances at once, sometimes behaving as though the Christian story is historically true, and sometimes as though it were true as symbolism illuminating the human condition. This only compounds the confusion and sometimes leads to children being taught as certainties (the existence of God; the divinity of Jesus) what are, in fact, hypothetical/symbolic attempts to explain man's existence and its relationship to the eternal.

Accordingly, the old message no longer carries its old conviction. The young – the big majority of them anyway –

find themselves unable to accept the Judaeo-Christian cosmology and ideology, simply because it does not fit in with knowledge current in the world around them. In contrast many of those in authority pretend that there is no problem except the fact that people are 'falling away' from old beliefs. The actual truth is that the old beliefs are falling away from modern knowledge. This is so for all the great religions represented in our multi-cultural world. So long as the pretence is kept up that everything is as it was before, there is no clear road to giving the young something to believe in on which they can found their lives. What is needed is not an attempt at a new set of absolutes but a perspective on the universe which gives meaning and dignity to life and a basis for putting together a set of values by which to live.

How far the young have already stepped out of the traditional religious beliefs was shown by one of the questions in the student questionnaire of which a part was described in Chapter 6. The question reads: 'What do you think are the two most important reasons of the following five for your resisting temptation to behave in a dishonest, unkind or selfish way? Please write (1) against the most important and (2) against the second most important:

(A) Because you want to live according to the principles of your religion?

(B) Because you do not want to lose the good opinion of your friends?

(C) Because you want to do as you would be done by?

(D) Because you fear that punishment or retaliation may follow?

(E) Because you feel such behaviour to be unworthy of you?

(The capital letters were not included in the questionnaire. They have been added for easy reference.)

The five choices represent different motivations for moral action: (A) represents the religious motive; (B) the social motive; (C) the motives of fellow-feeling, fair play and justice; (D) the expediency motive; and (E) the motive of self-respect. Results from the 943 returns, rounded off to avoid decimal places, were:

118

REASONS	(1ST AND 2ND)	%
AB	(religious/social)	2
AC	(religious/fair play)	7
AD	(religious/expediency)	1
AE	(religious/self-respect)	4
BA	(social/religious)	0
BC	(social/fair play)	3
BD	(social/expediency)	1
BE	(social/self-respect)	3
CA	(fair play/religious)	4
CB	(fair play/social)	8
CD	(fair play/expediency)	3
CE	(fair play/self-respect)	22
DA	(expediency/religious)	0
DB	(expediency/social)	2
DC	(expediency/fair play)	2
DE	(expediency/self-respect)	0
EA	(self-respect/religious)	3
EB	(self-respect/social)	6
EC	(self-respect/fair play)	21
ED	(self-respect/expediency)	3
Anomalous returns	(split choices etc.)	5

The motives of fellow-feeling (C) and self-respect (E) together account for 70% of first choices. (A), the religious choice, comes first in only 14% This is the more remarkable as Religious Education is compulsory in England and a strong suggestion goes along with this that moral behaviour derives from religious belief.

We must, of course, take account of the fact that choice (C) is the Goldren Rule which is stated in one way or another in all the great religions; nevertheless, it is a reason which is rooted in human feeling rather than in divine revelation; it is a human reason for behaving as a fully human being. Indeed, it has socio/biological force since it is hard to see how civilization could have evolved at all if the principles of

119

fellow-feeling, fair play and justice had not been respected in the early human communities that preceded the emergence of the great religions. Religion in its positive role can then be seen as defending and confirming right human behaviour rather than as initiating it. This is a reversal of the original Christian belief that man was without 'grace' by nature and could only attain virtue by divine intervention.

Not only ideas about the source of virtue but also the meaning of the word 'God' have been changing in the modern era, and in the minds of the young. One of the most thorough inquiries into religious orientation in Great Britain was conducted by the Opinion Research Centre for the Independent Television Authority. The views analysed were collected from a random sample of 1,071 adults (sixteen plus) in the first week of February, 1968. This showed a 50/50 balance between those who were certain of their belief in God and those who were uncertain. A significant finding was that certainty of belief in God declined steadily from the oldest age group to the youngest. The range of change was:

BELIEF IN GOD	RESPONDENTS IN AGE GROUP 16–24	RESPONDENTS IN AGE GROUP 55–64
Certain	37%	60%
Uncertain	63%	40%

The actual conception of God also varied. The Church of England sample and the Roman Catholic one gave these results for Britain:

CONCEPT OF GOD	CHURCH OF ENGLAND %	ROMAN CATHOLIC %
A person	38	59
Some kind of impersonal power	46	19
Other answers and don't knows	16	22

A teacher in a comprehensive school thought she would like to find out what the fifth form students (aged fifteen plus) in her school believed. She put to the class the question: 'What is your idea of God?' and asked the students to write their replies anonymously on pieces of paper which were provided. The question was included among others in order to avoid over-emphasis on a particular question. The following is a selection from the variety of views that emerged:

I imagine God as an immense power in the form of an aged man who is wise.

My idea of God is someone to look up to like a second father, who I feel can always help when anything is wrong.

God is a person.

God is not a person but he is there in some form.

God is some kind of spirit.

I imagine God as the power of creation, personified by goodness and love.

God is an impersonal perfection.

God is the perfect being if he is alive, otherwise I don't know.

I can't imagine God.

I don't know what it is like or even if there is one.

I don't believe in God.

It seems clear that traditional religious beliefs are no longer being accepted as absolutes by the younger generation in spite of the social pressures exerted to preserve them intact. Educationally, this leaves us with three urgent problems:

1. What perspective on life and the universe can we offer to young people which will carry conviction for them and help them to see their lives as significant?

2. Where can we find a source of values which young and old, as well as people of different nationalities and backgrounds, can share as the social/moral basis for our schools and other communities?

3. How can we fill the 'inspiration gap' now that religious belief is no longer a source of self-transcendence except for

a minority of youth?

These three questions are really different aspects of a single problem – how to offer an orientation to existence that is consistent with contemporary knowledge and which has a good chance of accommodating the new knowledge that will certainly come pouring in during the years immediately ahead.

Let us make a start at framing such an orientation. If we look straight at what we know, the only appropriate response is sheer wonder and astonishment at the facts of existence. We live on a tiny planet in an immense universe which seems, nevertheless, to be one unified whole, a vast continuum. This universe is structured from, and operates by, energy manifesting itself in many forms. Matter itself, as we have known since Einstein's famous $E = MC^2$, is energy organized into structures of various sizes and complexities: molecular complexes, molecules, atoms and sub-atomic 'particles'. From these, all that exists is made. Everything that goes on is also energy in some form – the Earth moving round the sun, the spluttering of a match, the waves of the sea, the growth of a plant, the movement of an animal, the thoughts and feelings of people. All are manifestations of energy in action. They are not *only* energy in action because they are qualitatively different from each other, but without energy none of them could be. The Earth receives a huge input of energy from the sun and balances the energy account by infra-red radiation from its dark side.

Energy in movement from source to output is the engine of nature. One of the things that this energy transition creates is life itself, when conditions are right for the elaboration of protein molecules, upon which all living creatures depend. The main elements from which these molecules of life are formed are plentiful so that things are ready for the emergence of life once the conditions are favourable. Ninety-eight per cent of a human being is composed of carbon, hydrogen, nitrogen, oxygen, phosphorus and sulphur. Add calcium and fifteen trace elements and that makes up the odd two per cent. The chemical composition of plants is much the same – after all, we can live on them! What turns out to make the difference is not the building blocks but their arrangement. We live in a world of infinitely varying patterns. Energy seems to become elaborated into as many forms as circumstances permit, the forms attaining whatever complexity the situation makes possible.

One aspect of this incredible elaboration of energy patterns is the evolution of the multitudes of living forms, which change and adapt to fit any niche that they can find to fill. We human beings are the inheritors of three thousand million years of this evolutionary process. As the dominant species on this planet because of our high, acquired adaptability, we are now more involved in psychological, social and cultural evolution than in biological change, but we are still evolving nevertheless. Within this complex mosaic of matter and life is contained an incredible potential for change. Man has himself used this potential to develop hitherto unknown species of animals and plants and has even constructed entirely new materials out of the building blocks of the universe, of which plastics are one example. We are, in this century, beginning to manipulate the basic structures of nature. This is an awesome responsibility with future outcomes that it is impossible to predict.

Modern man finds himself to be a creative organization of energy, and a self-conscious being at that, within an infinitely energetic and creative universe. We are, as Sir Bernard Lovell put it, 'in the centre of immensities'. We find ourselves to be the eyes and ears and thinking of the universe as we struggle to make sense of it all. And we now have such knowledge and power that we can destroy the very life-systems on this planet – of which we are ourselves a part – if we do not act with sufficient concern and imagination to match our modern powers. We have the inescapable responsibility of being the custodians of planet earth. This responsibility, arising from contemporary technology, is an entirely new commitment for mankind.

Yet we still have no explanation of existence itself. Neither theologians nor scientists have a satisfactory answer to offer. Some seek explanations in terms of natural and supernatural forces interacting with one another; others see the whole as one elaborately complex Nature about whose intricacies we are slowly gaining knowledge, even though we stand only on the fringes of understanding. Either way, it is certain that we live in the presence of a profound conundrum. It is an enigmatic background to our lives. But we do have a situation to deal with – the situation of Being, as a person, and the situation of responsibility for the planet. To be ourselves fully and responsibly there are all kinds of explorations to be attempted: the search outwards into the world and the universe; the search inwards into the depths of our own being; and the search to fulfil ourselves by interacting effectively with the world of people and things around us. We grow whole by accepting commitment to all these modes of being. The certainty has gone, but the search will always be there because man's consciousness is raised as he gains in knowledge and understanding so that he will always be wanting to grasp what lies beyond his reach. To quote Sir Bernard Lovell again: 'the pursuit of understanding is a transcendent value in man's life and purpose.'

Such is the pattern of our human reality which it is our task to share with the young. I cannot believe that this 'mighty sum of things', which manifests itself through infinite energy, potential, wonder and beauty, as well as through our own being, does not carry within it enough excitement and inspiration to engage the imagination of the young, and lift their awareness from absorption with the trivial into a sense of the deeper implications of existence, and so give significance to their lives. Modern youth are themselves eager to pursue the endless quest; it is they who have become engrossed by ideas of exploring inner space and consciousness raising.

An inept deficiency in education is the lack of any serious attempt on the part of our schools to convey a sense of the exciting realities now opening up before us. Of the student sample (Chapter 6) ninety-two per cent had been taught nothing about astronomy during their last two years at school. The fascinating story of evolution is usually put across as an aspect of biology, not as the dynamics of nature's splendour, and a continuing factor in human life. Or again, many children leave school without any awareness of the human being's symbiotic relationship with the planet, or even that we are all totally dependent on the sun and the soil for our food. One teacher commented: 'We aren't giving them any sort of vision. Expediency can never be inspiring.' Thus, the wonders of existence are commonly ignored.

By such glaring omissions, we deprive young people of a modern perspective, and then complain that they are cynical, apathetic and materialistic. One of the best antidotes to cynicism, apathy and materialism today is an imaginative grasp of the nature and responsibilities of human existence within the context of evolution on this planet. We see this demonstrated in one form in the spread of ecological morality in the world; the struggle between those who care for the planet and those who only care about exploiting it. A minority of schools are doing something towards developing ecological understanding but the majority seem to be blind to its social and moral importance.

Not only ecological values, but human values also emerge naturally from an education which deals properly with the human condition. Basic moral values – telling truth to one another, being honest, caring, compassion and concern, a dedication to justice and fair play, responsibility – are really just the names that humanity has created to identify what are the essential values of human relationships. Happy personal relationships and effective social organization are impossible unless such values can be assumed to be operative. Moral values are, in fact, as pragmatic as the values of nutrition. Either you respect them and thrive, as a person or society, or you ignore them and grow sick. A school that is honest about the human situation, that conveys the challenge and excitement of existence, that surrounds children with a community in which the human values are constantly in evidence, and that helps children to make contact with great lives and great human achievements, will be doing for the modern child what religious absolutism did for earlier generations – making it clear what moral values are and why they matter. Today the young will not receive moral values as precepts; they need, rather, to learn them through encounter with life, and through the moral content of the subjects they learn.

The logic of our times is that we should help children to acquire a contemporary perspective on the universe, the world, the human species and the responsibilities that go with our humanity. Our educational purpose should be to invite the young to join in the adventure of mankind in a way that stirs their imagination and altruism. Religious education has its place in this because religion has been one of man's ways of coming to terms with the fundamentals of existence – creation, birth, life, death, eternity – but it can no longer expect to occupy the central position it once did. In the modern world, religion has to take its place along with science, the arts and philosophy as ways of striving for truth and relationship; it has no special claim to certainty. Religion should, therefore, *not* be presented as the supreme source of human goodness and values. This is a fatal error today because children may be brought to consider religion and values as a single package, and to believe themselves to be free from moral obligations when the religious beliefs propounded within society and school cease to carry conviction. Furthermore, religions are by their nature divisive so that a common ground for social/moral behaviour needs an independent basis in human values derived directly from the human situation. Today, we have to work towards a social/ moral framework which is valid for all the world. The struggle to get the Universal Declaration of Human Rights honoured globally is one step in this direction; others will have to be taken in their turn.

The young are longing for commitment, hence their tendency to identify with all kinds of cults and hero figures. Yet they cannot become committed within a vacuum. The schools are failing the younger generation because in outlook as well as curriculum they are harking back to traditional ways and ideas that have lost their impact. One feature of this is an outmoded authoritarianism in the presentation of values. It used to be thought that, in perspective and values, the adults knew while the young were expected to listen. Now we know that nobody knows with that much certainty.

126

And the society around us is hardly convincing evidence to the young of the older generation's particular wisdom. Many of the young people around the world are in revolt against the materialistic values of the catch-as-catch-can society. They are looking for something more fulfilling. Young and old, we are in the search together – for ourselves, for relationships, for understanding. In this search, as in everything else, the appropriate bond between teachers and students today is the bond of shared humanity as they move forward in partnership towards the future.

12

FIT FOR THE FUTURE

The hosts of young people at present busily engaged in our schools in their various struggles with tests and examinations are destined to find themselves by their middle adult years in a society unrecognizably different from the one to which we have become accustomed. What lies ahead is revolutionary change resulting not from political but technological transformation, even though there will certainly be profound political consequences as well. The schools do not seem to be awake to this future and the need to prepare children for it, not only by teaching them about it, but also by helping them to become the sort of people who can deal with it – as individuals and as citizens. The dominance of the teaching-testing routines makes for inward-looking school communities which pay too little attention to the changing world outside.

The most spectacular aspect of tomorrow's world is the much publicized 'microprocessing revolution'. In a sentence, this means that, increasingly, people will not be wanted for much of the work that they do at present. Some kinds of work will still go on, even expand – social services, communications and transport for example – but thousands of jobs will cease to exist. Exactly how that will turn out in practice no one can predict. New careers will emerge. But more spare time for more people is sure to be one consequence since the alternative to a shorter working day will be an intolerably high level of unemployment. We have to imagine a society with something like a five hour working day and a four day working week. People who lack inner

128

resources to organize their lives for personal fulfilment, rather than for the accumulation of money and possessions, will be highly vulnerable in such a society. The higher quality of life of which we hear a good deal these days needs to be matched by people capable of creating it and enjoying it. A nightmare situation is not impossible in which millions of the population are driven to despair by meaningless idleness while other millions are drawn into the social services in an effort to shore up the multitude of broken lives – we can see the beginnings of that already.

This aspect of the future world calls for very much more than education for leisure; it urgently requires education in the meaningful use of personal powers, in establishing all kinds of growing points within individual experience during school years that can be developed further in later life. Education for work – which may take many different forms during a lifetime – will still be important, but, as of now, a major role for the schools should be not just to teach students how to earn a living but how to live. In the society to come, Professor Tom Stonier has predicted, we shall need only 10% of the labour force to supply our basic needs – foodstuffs, raw materials and manufactured goods. This envisages a vast switch in work-style and life-style in the future. Flexibility, competence as people, and lifelong learning will become essential for survival in private life and in careers.

The microprocessing revolution will multiply by many times the economic and monetary problems already shaking the world. The present system which depends on profitable scarcity and is upset by abundance – even of food in a half-starved world – will somehow have to be regenerated into a system that can handle plenty. As a part of this, world cooperation in production and distribution will ultimately have to replace the existing style of ruthless and wasteful competition. There will also have to be cooperation in conserving resources, including the environment. The young need to be alerted to these transformations.

A related problem which will come to a head within the next fifteen years will be the refusal of the nations producing primary products to go on suffering a low standard of living while the wealthiest third of the world continue to cream off advantages for themselves. If the gross disparity is not corrected, the world will explode under the stress. Young people now in school will be caught up in the many adaptations that will have to be made one way or another. If they are not taught about the realities of their world, and the nature of its inter-dependence, they will be hopelessly unprepared when the crises of readjustment begin to bite. The ultimate end *can* be a world of shared prosperity. Intermediately the equalizing process is sure to be fraught with difficulties.

Another shock wave for the future is the information revolution which is, even now, gathering way. The adolescents of this generation will grow up into a world when up-dated information on an increasing range of subjects will be available at will from terminals attached to the television or telephone. For a fee, we shall be linked up to the world memory bank – a vast electronic extension of the individual human brain. Many other new sources of information will also be readily available. The master-minds of tomorrow will not be those who retain within their heads, for instant recall, masses of factual information but the people skilful at selecting and relating information. Relating information is, we should notice, an intuitive right-hemisphere function.

The information revolution has a sinister aspect. The facts of our personal lives, or considerable parts of them, will be stored in official memory banks of one kind or another – health statistics, credit records, personal interests, family situations, where we went on holiday last year, etc, etc. This will give officialdom a greatly inflated power unless people are constantly vigilant to preserve their privacy and independence. Hence, the necessary concomitant to the information and silicon chip revolutions will have to be a sharpened individual alertness combined with a vigorous grassroots democracy. Once again, we are brought back to the quality of people. The human quality of people will matter in the future as it has never mattered before. The powerful structure of technological society will need the balance of self-confident, imaginative individuals. The race is on, as H. G. Wells predicted long ago, between education and catastrophe; catastrophe in the form of a kid-glove 1984; a controlling élite of computer people, technicians and manipulators, with bread and circuses, modern style, for the masses, who would exist in a state of perpetual confusion about who or what was controlling their lives.

All such trends make a thorough understanding of what is going on, and what the options are, vital. We cannot build a human future for mankind on a foundation of ignorance. In the new revolution there will be no defence against the élites except through the awareness of the community, and the proper education of those who form the élites.

How can ordinary people be kept in the know at a time when, among other things, a knowledge explosion is also taking place? At present, specialisms are fragmenting the corpus of human knowledge. No specialist can keep track of what is going on in his own field let alone what is happening in others. We long ago reached the point when the languages of the specialisms precluded ready communication between their exponents. It is extremely dangerous socially for this state of affairs to continue indefinitely. We have to become an intercommunicating society. The trained intelligence of the future will have to be more like that of a new-style Renaissance Man – informed on all fronts – rather than that of the one-subject specialist cut off in his academic insularity. This is not to imply a dilution of specialist study, but that the time has come for specialists to leave their ivory towers and join the human race.

To socialize learning, we shall have to organize it in networks rather than in encapsulated cells. This will enable the specialist in one field to gain entry into the others, while the 'well-informed citizen' can acquire a generalized knowledge of them all. The motivation for this will come from sustaining every individual's natural curiosity. People want to know. It is the task of educators to put knowledge into forms that permit a ready grasp of the basic ideas.

Some specialists like to think that it is not desirable to let non-specialists share their knowledge, and denigrate as

131

'popularisers' those who seek to communicate specialist knowledge to non-specialists. This is a vanity which we can no longer afford. New knowledge always becomes general knowledge in the end. Gravity was thought to be an incomprehensible mystery at the time of Newton; now every child can grasp the idea. One role of future educators – and we should be starting on it now – will be to accelerate the speed at which new principles reach common understanding. There is, for example, nothing to prevent fourteen-year-olds of average ability understanding why we have to describe position and motion in space in terms of four dimensions; or grasping the general nature of the extraordinary world of quantum physics; or the principles of nutrition, or ecology or what you will. Such basic information is readily conveyed to children at the Royal Institution Christmas Lectures in a stimulating and exciting way. Every science department in every school should be engaged in similar activities. Learning made relevant to life is always exciting. We have to use all the skill and technology at our disposal to teach compellingly about man's total situation, including the economic bases of life in industry and agriculture.

The development of a general network of understanding is no longer to be considered as a frill to be added to specialist education if there is time; it is a necessary component in everyone's education. Both the schools and the media should be vigorously engaged in providing it. The greater the knowledge explosion, and the faster the spread of the information revolution, the greater the risk of domination by 'experts', if knowledge is not shared widely within the community. Moreover, fundamental knowledge adds richness to personal life.

I have discussed only what are virtual certainties for the future. There are also possibilities and complications by the dozen. The mind boggles at what may be in store for our children. Of this there can be no doubt: amid all the innovations and confusions that are to come, only versatile, flexible, self-confident individuals will be able to digest the changes, adapt to them, and control them.

To sum up: this book has been concerned with the development of whole young people for present and future life by the nourishment of their powers in the social context of a warm, friendly, purposeful school community. It has stressed that, while respecting the role of academic dedication in human advance, we must throw off the intense academic control of secondary education as too narrow, rigid and abstract for the burgeoning adolescent phase of growth. Intuition, imagination, creativity, social awareness, a coherent perspective, a caring outlook and moral insight are every bit as important as subjects and skills in the education of individuals, and in the maintenance of a civilized society. In order to secure this, the schools have to educate the functions of the right-hemisphere mode of consciousness as carefully as the left-hemisphere mode.

It has also been emphasized that adolescents become submerged and broken – or aggressively hostile – if their confidence is shattered by too much failure. This fact alone discredits our present system of secondary education which, by its very nature, generates failure. Confidence is to be built – along with motivation – by bringing out the actual potentialities of the particular child within a stimulating school environment that tempts the child to explore what he is and to build on what he can do, with the guidance and encouragement of the teacher. This is the path to an assured self-awareness and confidence. Assessment should be a continuous part of this process, in which pupil and teacher both share, and not a dreaded trip-wire at the end of the course.

We have seen that good ideas abound about how to improve education but that very little gets done to implement these ideas. The reason for this is not only the academic illusion, sustained by its armoury of examinations, but also the attempt to fill the obvious gaps in secondary education by an additive approach. What is needed is more synthesis in education – replacing isolated subjects by confluent education which continuously nourishes the range of personal powers while, *pari passu*, converting the curriculum from a patchwork of abstractions into a coherent pattern of understanding. The basic principle here is that all learning should be rooted in life.

133

In Chapter 5, we drew attention to a serious omission in most secondary education – failure to pay sufficient attention to the development of personal competence. What we see in regard to this important function of education is plenty of good intentions unsupported by effective action. Yet capability as a human being lies at the heart of success in living. The neglect of education for general competence as a person is further evidence of the fatal gap that exists between education and life. To close that gap we have to reorient secondary education so that it continuously fosters curiosity, confidence, social awareness, and the experience of responsible involvement with others.

Throughout the book, the case has been made for bringing adolescents and adults into a closer partnership. The ticket of admission to the adolescents' world is that we accept and work through the dynamics of their own lives; their vigour, their sexual awakening, their love of change, mobility and excitement, their interests and hopes. The necessary partnership of purpose between teachers and pupils has – if there is to be a fruitful cooperation within the school community – to be as firmly secured between teachers and the less-able scholars as between the high fliers and those who guide their studies. By not sufficiently respecting the personal abilities, interests and aspirations of the less-able academically we are both destroying their capacity for life and generating barbarism within society. Educational failure is a seed-bed for vandalism, destructiveness and crime.

We have further noted that secondary schools today have assiduously to help young people to acquire, by the relationships and experiences provided within the school, and through links with the wider community, a valid perspective on the modern world, a feeling of involvement in the human adventure, a sense of wonder about existence, and an understanding of those values upon which personal and social life depend. This, too, is best achieved by a search together, a sharing of our common humanity.

What does all this add up to in economic terms – the perennial 'can we afford it?' question? Many of these vitally necessary changes are changes of heart and direction that cost nothing. Any school that means business can start on them tomorrow; some already have.

But, in addition to a new sense of purpose, our secondary schools must be given the human resources they need to do the job properly. Falling rolls are offering a real opportunity greatly to improve the staff-pupil ratios in our secondary schools. The opportunity must not be missed. We cannot build a good future for individuals, or the nation, on an under-educated and, often, miseducated community. Either we put capital into generating whole, effective people or we shall be forced to spend untold millions on difficult and often unsuccessful attempts to rehabilitate those whose personal adequacy and sense of social responsibility have been undermined rather than developed by the education they have received. This is as true of the wealthy who get caught with their hands in the till as it is of the feckless incompetents. How either got that way is as much an educational question as a psychological one. Similarly for all inept, hostile, and dishonest lives. It is nonsense to say that the schools cannot be held responsible for failures in life. The schools are not totally responsible, but responsible they certainly are. They do not hesitate to claim credit for their successes.

It follows that the greatest care has to be taken in the selection and training of teachers, especially head teachers. Teachers have to be specialists in the dynamics of individual development just as much as masters of specific subject skills. Inquiries on both sides of the Atlantic suggest that between twelve and thirty per cent of adolescents do not feel able to turn to their parents with their personal problems. This group, especially, need all the understanding and support they can get at school. So every teacher has to be ready to play a role as guide and friend as well as teacher. He, or she, will also be often called upon to act as a model, a person with whom young people can identify. Because of this, teachers should be competent in life as well as knowledgeable in subjects. They should be life-loving, life-affirming personalities. This will be even more important in the future than it is at present.

Since teachers have a big share of the responsibility for

135

the personal growth of the coming generation, they should, obviously, be selected and trained with that in mind. If we are to have a mature society, the nation must be prepared to pay for both the right quality and the right quantity of teachers to do the job, and to provide plenty of in-service training to keep the profession refreshed and up-to-date. An ungenerous staff-pupil ratio and efficient in-service training are totally inconsistent with one another. Many in-service training courses are under-subscribed because the teachers who would like to attend cannot be spared from school duties.

To fail to capitalize adequately the proper education of the coming generation is, at this time in our history, the economics of national suicide.

There is still a great deal of educational research crying out for attention, but we already have enough insight to transform secondary education from a bundle of past habits into an efficient and humane system. It is a matter of clarifying aims and willing means, and constantly evaluating what is happening, in human as well as in academic terms.

We need a vigorous, concerted drive to raise the overall educational quality of the secondary schools. Shall we as individuals, and as a nation – especially teachers, parents, inspectors and administrators – really apply ourselves to this task, *for all of our young people*, or are we proposing to go on feeding to coming generations bread that is buttered on both sides for some, dry on both sides for others and, for almost all, lacking in essential vitamins? We have not long in which to decide and to act. Educationally and socially it is almost certainly later than we think.

REFERENCES

The following are the books and papers which form the principal sources of reference for this book, excluding those for which details are given in the text itself. The books and papers are listed in the order in which material from them is featured in the chapters.

CHAPTER 2

Morton-Williams, R. & Finch, S., *Enquiry I: Young School Leavers*, an investigation carried out by the Schools Council. London, Her Majesty's Stationery Office, 1968, p. 214.

Adler, Alfred, *What Life Should Mean To You*. London, Allen & Unwin, 1932.

Mayer, Iona & Philip, 'Socialization by Peers: the Youth Organization of the Red Xhosa' in Mayer, Philip (Ed.) *Socialization, the Approach from Social Anthropology*. London, Tavistock Publications, 1970, pp. 159 – 189.

Kenyatta, Jomo, *Facing Mount Kenya*. London, Secker & Warburg, 1938, p. 158.

(Note)

The overlap in perceptions of teachers, parents and students concerning education for personal maturity is reported in *Enquiry 1*, op. cit. p. 53 and in Raven, John, *Education, Values and Society* (see Chapter 5) pp. 56, 65 – 68 and 92.

CHAPTER 3

Rosenthal, Robert, *Pygmalion in the Classroom*. New York,

Holt, Rinehart and Winston, 1968.

Pilling, D. and Kellmer Pringle, M., *Controversial Issues in Child Development*, Paul Elek, 1978.

Hargreaves, D. *Social Relations in a Secondary School*. London, Routledge and Kegan Paul, 1967, Chapter 5.

Clegg, Sir Alec, *The Achievements of the Education Service 1870 – 1970*. Lecture delivered at Central Hall, Westminster, 1 May, 1970.

Bruner, Jerome, *Toward a Theory of Instruction*. New York, Norton, 1968, p. 101.

Hoffman, Banesh, *Einstein*. London, Paladin, 1975, p. 222.

Curriculum 11 – 16, working papers by Her Majesty's Inspectorate. London, 1977, p. 6.

Musgrove, F., *Youth and the Social Order*. London, Routledge and Kegan Paul, 1964.

Orr, Sir David, 'Training as an Investment' in *BACIE Journal*, December, 1978.

Jarratt A. A., 'Educated for What' in *BACIE Journal*, December, 1975.

Report on National Engineering Scholarships, *The Guardian*, 25 October, 1978.

Wall, W. D., *Constructive Education for Adolescents*. London, UNESCO and Harrap, 1977, p. 196.

CHAPTER 4

Penfield, Wilder, *The Mystery of the Mind*. Princeton University Press, 1975.

Bruner, Jerome, *Relevance of Education*. London, Penguin, 1974, p. 101.

Ornstein, Robert E., *The Psychology of Consciousness*. New York, Harcourt Brace Jovanovich, 1977.

Sperry, R. W., 'Lateral specialization of cerebral function in the surgically separated hemispheres' in McGuigan, F. J. (Ed.), *The Psychophysiology of Thinking*. New York, Academic Press, 1973.

Nebes, Robert D., 'Man's So-Called Minor Hemisphere' in Wittrock, M.C. (Ed.), *The Human Brain*. New Jersey, Pentice-Hall, 1977, pp. 97–106.

Bogen, Joseph E., 'Some Educational Implications of Hemi-sphere Specialization' in Wittrock M. C. (Ed.), *The Human Brain*. op. cit. pp. 133–152.

Gazzaniga, Michael S., 'Review of the Split Brain' in *The Human Brain*, op. cit. pp. 89–96.

Read, Herbert, *Education Through Art*. London, Faber and Faber, 1943.

Witkin, Robert W., *The Intelligence of Feeling*. London, Heinemann, 1974.

Ross, Malcolm, *The Creative Arts*. London, Heinemann, 1978.

Blackburn, Thomas, 'Sensuous-Intellectual Complement-arity in Science' in Ornstein Robert (Ed.), *The Nature of Human Consciousness*. San Francisco, W. H. Freeman, 1973.

CHAPTER 5

Raven, John, *Education, Values and Society: The Objectives of Education and the Nature and Development of Com-petence*. London, H. K. Lewis and New York, The Psychological Corporation, 1977, Chapter X.

Raven, John, 'Perceptions of, and Reactions to the Educa-tional System and their Implications for Policy' in *Studies in Educational Evaluation*, vol 4, No. 1, pp. 31–45.

Kellmer Pringle, Mia, *The Needs of Children*. London, Hutchinson, 1975.

CHAPTER 6

Sixth-Form Citizens, an inquiry of the Schools Committee of the Association For Education in Citizenship. Oxford University Press, 1950, pp. 170–199.

The Curriculum of the Open Sixth, General Studies Associ-ation Research Report, 1976, p. 4.

Goodman, Paul, *Growing Up Absurd*. New York, Random House, 1956.

Illich, Ivan, *Deschooling Society*. London, Calder & Boyars, 1971.

Holt, John, *Instead of Education*. London, Penguin, 1977.

CHAPTER 7

Such a vast literature exists on curriculum development that a list fully supportive of the various ideas in vogue would be impossibly long. The following five books give the gist of developments in Britain.

Hirst, P. H. and Peters, R. S. *The Logic of Education*, Routledge and Kegan Paul, London 1970 and de Bono, *Teaching Thinking*, Pelican Books, 1978.

The Whole Curriculum 13–16, Schools Council Working Paper 53. London, Evans/Methuen Educational, 1975.

MacDonald, B. and Walker, R., *Changing The Curriculum*. London, Open Books, 1976.

Education in Schools: A Consultative Document, Her Majesty's Stationery Office, 1977.

Kelly, A. V., *The Curriculum: Theory and Practice*. London, Harper & Row, 1977.

Dore, Ronald, *The Diploma Disease*. London, Allen & Unwin, 1976.

Submission by the National Association of Head Teachers to the Welsh Under-Secretary as reported in *The Guardian*, 27 November, 1978.

Sixth Form Syllabuses and Examinations: a New Look, Schools Council Research Studies. London, Macmillan Education, 1976, p. 12.

Holt, John, op. cit. (see Chapter 6) p. 28.

Panufnik, Andrzej, *Impulse and Design in My Music*. London, Boosey & Hawkes, 1974.

Adibe, Nasrine, 'A call for more Confluent Education and a clarification of the term', in *Journal of the Society for Education Reconstruction*, vol. 6, No. 2, pp. 43–45.

Piaget, Jean, *The Psychology of Intelligence*. London, Routledge and Kegan Paul, 1950, p. 6.

Russell, James, *Change and Challenge in American Education*. Boston, Houghton Mifflin, 1965, pp. 47–48.

CHAPTER 8

Price, Christopher, 'What's going wrong in our schools?', *Times Educational Supplement*, 2 March, 1973.

Morton-Williams, R., Finch, S., op. cit. (see Chapter 1) p. 60.

Raven, John, 'School Rejection and its Amelioration' in *Educational Research*, vol. 20, No. 1, p. 4.

Fogelman, Ken (Ed), *Britain's Sixteen-Year-Olds*. London, National Children's Bureau, 1976, p. 51.

O'Hagan, F. J., 'Attitudes of Offenders and Non-Offenders Towards School', in *Educational Research*, vol. 19, No. 2, pp. 142–146.

Boyle, Jimmy, *A Sense of Freedom*. London, Pan Books, 1977, p. 34.

Millham, Spencer, 'The Dustbin Men', a lecture given at the Dartington Educational Conference, May, 1976.

Kellmer Pringle, Mia, *The Roots of Violence and Vandalism*. London, National Children's Bureau, 1973.

Piaget, Jean, *The Construction of Reality in the Child*. New York, Basic Books, 1954, pp. 350–386.

Huxley, Sir Julian, 'Transhumanism', in *New Bottles for New Wine*. London, Chatto & Windus, 1957, p. 15.

Hodgkin, R. A., *Born Curious*. New York, John Wiley & Sons, 1976.

Kellmer Pringle, Mia, op. cit. (see Chapter 5)

Blackham, H. J. (Ed.) *Education For Personal Autonomy*, National Council of Social Service, 1978.

Yoshiki, N., *For Full Development of Human Potential*, Lifelong Integrated Education Centre, Japan, 1978.

CHAPTER 9

Jencks, Christopher, *Inequality*. London, Penguin Books, 1975, p. 134.

Peters, R. S., *Ethics and Education*. London, Allen and Unwin, 1966, Chapter XI.

Cole, L. & Nelson Hall, I., *Psychology of Adolescence*. London, Holt, Rinehart & Winston, 1970, pp. 578–579.

Bailey, John R., 'Implicit Moral Education in Secondary Schools' in *Journal of Moral Education*, vol. 8, No. 1, pp. 32–40.

Raven, John, op. cit. (see Chapter 5) pp. 72–75.

Ten Good Schools: A Secondary School Inquiry, conducted

by members of Her Majesty's Inspectorate. London, Her Majesty's Stationery Office, 1977, p. 36.

Rutter, M., Maughan, B., Mortimore, P., and Ouston, J., *Fifteen Thousand Hours*, Open Books, 1979.

CHAPTER 10

Frayn, Michael, a comment reported in 'To Sir with gratitude' in *Telegraph Sunday Magazine*, 27 August, 1978.

Hipkin, John, 'The case for exam reform' in Jackson, Brian and McAlhone, Beryl (Eds.) *Verdict on The Facts*. Cambridge, Advisory Centre For Education, pp. 48–52.

Klug, Brian, 'Profile Alternatives to Grading' in Upton, Lawrence (Ed.), *An Examination of Assessment*. London, NUS Publications, 1974, pp. 28–32.

Cox, Roy, 'Alternatives to the three hour examinations' in *An Examination of Assessment*. op. cit. p. 15.

Ayckbourn, Alan, in an interview with John Heilpern, in the programme for '*Bedroom Farce*'. London, Prince of Wales Theatre, 1978.

Wall, W. D., op. cit. (see Chapter 3) p. 149.

Burgess Tyrrell, *Education After School*. London, Penguin, 1977, pp. 147–167.

CHAPTER 11

Religion in Britain and Northern Ireland. London, Independent Television Authority, 1970.

Shklovskii, I. S., & Sagan, Carl, *Intelligent Life in the Universe*. London, Pan Books, 1977, p. 345.

Morowitz, H. J., *Energy Flow in Biology*. New York, Academic Press, 1968.

Lovell, Sir Bernard, 'In The Centre of Immensities', Presidential Address to the 137th. Annual Meeting of the British Association for the Advancement of Science, printed in *The Advancement of Science*, August, 1975.

CHAPTER 12

Stonier, Tom, 'Educating for the Future' in *The Listener*, 28 September, 1978.

Stonier, Tom, 'Technological change and the future', a paper given to the British Association, September, 1979.

142

Elias, J., *High School Youth Look at their Problems*. Washington, the College Bookshop, 1949.

(Note)

The proportion of English adolescents unlikely to turn to their parents for help with personal problems is suggested by, as yet, unpublished returns from the inquiry described in Chapter 6. This gives 12% for female students and 29% for male students.

INDEX

144

146